FEB 1 8 2011

Praise for *Lead, Sell, or Get Out of the Way*

"Strap yourself onto a sales booster rocket and read Ron Karr's newest book, *Lead, Sell, or Get Out of the Way*. Karr is the expert who gives you a guaranteed approach to growing your company's sales beyond your wildest dreams. I know, as he has done it for mine. I promise you this book will increase your sales exponentially."
—*Don Gabor*, author of *Turn Small Talk into Big Deals*

"Karr's book, *Lead, Sell, or Get Out of the Way*, illustrates what we believe: that knowing your customers' needs is the single most important factor in building sales. Business starts with the sale. To make profitable sales, you need to understand your customer and create a timely value proposition. This book shows you how to do both."
—*Larry Kellner*, chairman and CEO, Continental Airlines

"As CEO and Chairman of the Board of three publicly traded companies, I felt that Karr's strategies in *Lead, Sell, or Get Out of the Way* absolutely provided the powerful results he predicted. In one case, we completely eliminated a competitor who posed a strategic threat. I guess you can say they 'got out of the way.' Karr will show you what is required and how to be a top producer in your market. This book is a must-read."
—*James T. Treace*, president & managing member, J&A Group, LLC, and former chairman of the board, Wright Medical, Inc. and Kyphon, Inc.

"Karr captures a lifetime of winning strategies and experiences and puts them in a practical context for sales leaders and sellers. This book challenges many of the older paradigms of selling and emphasizes the importance of keeping the focus on the customers and providing positive outcomes. In today's challenging market conditions, where the primary focus is on market share, this is a must-read."
—*Barry S. Goldstein*, senior vice president, Global Sales Strategy & Operations, Starwood Hotels & Resorts Worldwide, Inc.

"Karr's book clearly identifies what it takes to be a highly effective sales leader. The principles in Karr's book are concise and illuminating. Follow his system and your sales organization will succeed in any market. An absolute must-read."
—*Mike Beaudry*, division president, United Natural Foods (UNFI)

"Karr does it again! *Lead, Sell, or Get Out of the Way* gives you the ultimate approach to giving added value to customers and create value for yourself...The seven traits are what's needed in today's world, and this book is an outstanding guide to becoming proficient in all of them."
—*David Preng*, Preng & Associates, The Global Energy Search Leader

"Karr's new book drives home the message of listening to the voice of the customer in order to qualify their needs, which in turn allows you to tailor an offering that should produce the desired results. This is a practical guide for being successful in sales that requires the reader to understand Karr's seven principals in order to complete the commitment sections at the end of various chapters. It is especially timely given the current pressures of intensified global competition that all companies face today."

—*Bruce S. Fisher*, vice president, Global Marketing, Hayward Pool Products, a division of Hayward Industries

"Karr captures perfectly what's challenging sales professionals today—sales professionals themselves. He not only articulates the path to sales excellence, but the state of mind necessary to be successful. I have been taught a hundred different paths to building successful sales. How Karr got it down to seven was impressive. But he really gets it down to three: lead, sell, or get out of the way."

—*Patrick H. McEvoy*, president & CEO, Multi-Financial Securities Corporation

"If you need to make rain, you need to read this book!"

—*Daniel W. Sklar*, Senior Counsel, Nixon Peabody LLP

"Six years ago, I formed my own independent financial services company after a twenty-seven-year successful career with a major life insurance company. Karr's coaching was critical to my success. Any regrets? Yes; I only wish that I had met him ten years earlier! This book is a must-read for anyone who wants to be and stay a top producer."

—*Joel N. Greenberg*, founder, Principal Wealth Advisory Services LLC

LEAD, SELL, OR GET OUT OF THE WAY

The 7 Traits of Great Sellers

RON KARR

WILEY

John Wiley & Sons, Inc.

Published by John Wiley & Sons, Inc., Hoboken, New Jersey
Published simultaneously in Canada

Limit of Liability/Disclaimer of Warranty: While the publisher and author have used their best efforts
in preparing this book, they make no representations or warranties with respect to the accuracy or
completeness of the contents of this book and specifically disclaim any implied warranties of
merchantability or fitness for a particular purpose. No warranty may be created or extended by sales
representatives or written sales materials. The advice and strategies contained herein may not be
suitable for your situation. You should consult with a professional where appropriate. Neither the
publisher nor author shall be liable for any loss of profit or any other commercial damages, including
but not limited to special, incidental, consequential, or other damages.

For general information on our other products and services or for technical support, please contact
our Customer Care Department within the United States at (800) 762-2974, outside the United
States at (317) 572-3993 or fax (317) 572-4002.

Wiley also publishes its books in a variety of electronic formats. Some content that appears in print
may not be available in electronic books. For more information about Wiley products, visit our web
site at www.wiley.com.

Library of Congress Cataloging-in-Publication Data:

Karr, Ron.
  Lead, sell, or get out of the way : the 7 traits of great sellers / Ron Karr.
    p. cm.
  Includes bibliographical references and index.
  ISBN 978-0-470-40218-4 (cloth)
  1. Selling.   I. Title.

  HF5438.25.K367 2009
  658.85–dc22

                          2008045572

Printed in the United States of America

10 9 8 7 6 5 4

To My Two Ladies
My wife, Cindy—Thank you for being there at my side as a
friend, supporter, and collaborator. You are simply the best.

My daughter, Amanda—As this book teaches, remember
to always help others achieve the results they are after.
Dedicate yourself to this mantra and you will live a life full
of blessings and riches.

*In Memory of Miriam Karr, mother, mentor, friend, and advisor.
You are greatly missed, but your presence will always be felt.*

Contents

Acknowledgments

This book would not have been written if it weren't for the many clients who have given me the privilege and opportunity of working with them. It is easy to ask for advice; it is quite another to translate that advice into action. These individuals and organizations had the courage to try new things and the will to achieve better results. Their actions, stories, and results are the foundation from which this book was written. I thank them for their support and confidence.

As with any project, there are many people to thank behind the scenes. To my family and friends who have had to put up with me talking about this project, spending many nights working on it; thank you for your understanding and support.

To my friends at Wiley, without your support this book would not be possible. To Matt Holt, vice president and publisher: Thank you for pushing me to get my proposal in; you can be quite persuasive, and you have the great leadership abilities described in this book. Thank you to Dan Ambrosio, my editor; your support was and is invaluable to this project. To Christine Moore, my favorite development editor: What can I say? You made this process look and feel so easy. Same goes to Jessica Campilango; thank you for holding everything together and making sure it all came out on time. And to my friends in marketing and publicity, Christine Kim, Peter Knapp and Jocelyn Cordova-Wagoner, the team members who will take this creation and help introduce it to the world at large: Thank you for all you have done and will continue to do. To Lauren Freestone, my production editor: thank you for correcting all of my missteps and making me look good. My gratitude also goes out to Brian Boucher for his superb cover design.

Special thanks to Brandon Toropov for his valuable counsel. Brandon, your advice, suggestions, and assistance were invaluable. The same holds true for my numerous colleagues for their support.

Last, but most important, a big and special thank you goes out to you, the reader. You represent the successes that are yet to be realized. Thank you for the time you are putting in to read this book. My wish is for you to achieve a return on your investment that far exceeds your expectations.

Introduction

Leading the Way

This book's title—*Lead, Sell or Get Out of the Way*—reflects the reality that, in today's market, there is simply no room for followers, but there is plenty of room for leaders who are willing to create outcomes that others have not yet imagined.

> ### The Leader's Wisdom
>
> "A wise man will make more opportunities than he finds." —Sir Francis Bacon

The competition is intense. If you do not assume a leadership role when it comes to producing results for your clients and helping them succeed at a higher level, your competition will be happy to do it for you—and will eventually push you out of the way.

Whether you sell a product, a service, or an idea, you must be able to influence other people as leaders do. Sales leaders don't just sell products, services, or ideas, and they don't just beat the competition at the same offering. They don't even sell against their competition. They *raise the bar* by identifying previously unidentified opportunities, and they create whole new levels of performance for their customers. In turn, they achieve significantly higher levels of success than others. They are the masters of influence.

Your ability to sell more products and services in less time and at higher profit depends more on your ability to connect with and influence others about the *outcomes* you can deliver for them than it does on the actual product or service you are selling. For 30 years, I have proven this principle over and over again to my clients: What you are really selling is not products, services, or ideas, but *outcomes*—the results that people can expect from implementing your ideas and using your products and services.

This book is all about what works; it is not about theory. Everything I have laid out for you here has been successfully implemented by my clients and by yours truly. *Lead, Sell, or Get Out of the Way* is a summary of everything I have learned, executed, and shared with my clients about leadership selling over a period of three decades. My clients have achieved remarkable things with this kind of selling. So have I, and so can you.

Two Ways to Grow a Business

There are two ways to grow a business successfully. The first is to develop organically from within, and make the same mistakes that everyone else has made. Although many people have done well with this approach, many have failed as well. This manner of cultivating a business takes more time and is far more costly than the second way, which is *to acquire the knowledge and experience gained by other people.*

By taking this approach, you can avoid making the same mistakes that others did, and you can move forward at a quicker pace. This is what this book is meant to do: help you *sell more in less time at higher profit* by adopting the same principles that the most effective leaders use to sell, without having to make the same mistakes they made along the way.

Three Choices

In today's market, you have three basic choices.

- *You Can Lead*. You can establish a leadership role in your own life by taking full responsibility for your own outcomes and establishing an attitude of complete accountability.
- *You Can Sell*. You can use that leadership role in your sales career to build alliances that establish zones of strategic mutual benefit for you and others,
- *You Can Get Out of the Way*. In other words, you can make room for a competitor who is willing to do both of the things listed above. Make no mistake—that's what's on the horizon if you choose *not* to sell as a leader.

This book is designed to help you make the first two a reality and avoid the third altogether.

My mother, Miriam Karr, was a well-known economist and, eventually, a vice president of a large U.S. bank with offices in several countries. She made a name for herself by identifying and building business with emerging markets. She embraced choices one and two above, and she taught me at a very early age how to build businesses and make deals that produced OUTCOMES that were so powerful stakeholders could not afford to shut them down. In her case, that meant starting a counter-trade group for the bank that helped Third World countries find buyers for their products. These were deals on which commissions were paid—and a percentage of these commissions was applied by the bank to offset that particular Third World country's outstanding debt to the bank. Her ability to see this opportunity, put her ideas to work, and initiate powerful dialogues made everyone involved in her work a winner. The countries needed to find buyers for their products; the bank needed to write down its debt and improve its bottom line. My mother made both of these things possible by championing something I call the *Integrated Dialogue*™.

The Integrated Dialogue™

Leaders know that a one-sided conversation is not as likely to get people invested with them as allies as a powerful integrated dialogue is.

What exactly is an integrated dialogue? It's a conversation that you take full responsibility for initiating and guiding that draws people out and elicits their experiences. It's a conversation based on a vision and a sense of shared purpose that identifies previously unidentified opportunities.

An integrated dialogue instantly distinguishes you and your offering from the competition. This is exactly how my mother built her business unit in emerging markets for the bank. Whether you've been selling for 30 years or you just started yesterday, there is still something for you—for all of us—to learn about the way great sales leaders take on the responsibility of initiating and leading such a dialogue.

This kind of dialogue is what the very best sales professionals—sales leaders—use to give their customers something they couldn't possibly get from a long monologue, or a brochure, or the Internet. This conversation allows you to lead the process and establish yourself as a resource for everyone who comes in contact with you. The Internet and brochures are only capable of selling a transaction. You, on the other hand, represent the ability to create a powerful relationship, one that identifies whole new zones of mutual opportunity, addresses far-ranging issues, and positions you as an invaluable resource: a leader.

Leaders know that people don't want to be sold. They simply want someone who's responsible and accountable to help guide them through the buying process. They are not looking to buy products or services. They are looking for solutions to their problems. They are looking for positive OUTCOMES.

Over the years, I've been privileged to work with thousands of sales leaders—beginning with my mom—who established an integrated dialogue to share their vision, identify previously unimagined opportunities, build alliances, and guide people through the process of buying.

In this book, I reveal everything I have learned from those leaders. I share their case studies with you and show you exactly how the concepts were put into action.

Let's get started!

1 | The Case for Leadership

On October 1, 1989, my brother-in-law Dan resigned from his position as a junior partner at a well-established law firm. Upon hearing the news, I immediately called him to inquire whether he was crazy; he assured me that he was completely sane. I asked him, "Why on Earth would you leave this position when you're on the fast track to becoming a senior partner?" His answer caught me by surprise.

My brother-in-law explained to me that he had a choice: He could continue working really hard and take only a small portion of the fees he brought in, or he could start his own firm, hire lawyers under him, and increase his share of the profits.

Dan knew one of the secrets of sales leadership.

> **The Leader's Advantage**
>
> You will make much more money through the efforts of others than you ever could make solely through your own efforts.

Most of the sales executives whom I encounter face the same choice that my brother-in-law faced—but don't realize it. They have not yet learned about sales leadership.

Beyond the Lone Ranger

Whether you are selling an idea, professional service, or a product, you are probably hoping to sell more this quarter than you did last quarter, in less time, and at a higher profit. *You cannot do this on your own, if indeed you ever could.* To hit the targets you now face, you must build and sustain coalitions that will support you and act on your behalf. The "Lone Ranger" selling model may have worked in the past; in fact, many successful Lone Rangers were promoted to sales managers. Unfortunately, what made them successful as a Lone Ranger sometimes becomes their biggest obstacle to success as a sales manager—namely, their inability to get things done through other people.

Nowadays, whether you are a top-producing salesperson, a salesperson who's trying to improve, a sales manager, or a professional services provider, you should know that the "Lone Ranger" selling model is a concept of the past. To succeed in business today, you must leverage the support and help of others. This book will show you how.

Leaders Don't Puke

Let's start with something you probably already know: Customers today don't want to be sold. In fact, the moment they feel they are being sold, they head for the hills—either by disengaging from the sales process or by simply ending the conversation, either audibly or silently. What customers *do* want is help in making the right choices. They don't need you to puke up all the features that your products and services have to offer.

You may wonder why I use the word "puke." Well, for starters, it's memorable. Members of my audiences tend to keep the "don't puke" rule in mind for a long time after I share it with them. Second, the word perfectly describes the basic problem we're looking at: When you puke up all the features you have to offer, you spray lots of junk around, you make a pretty big mess, and people try to avoid you afterwards. This idea of puking connects to one of the biggest mistakes that some salespeople make: They educate prospects, but don't sell very many of them.

The Leader's Advantage

PUKE stands for: People who Utter Knowledge about Everything.

About 10 years ago, a prominent fashion designer was seeking advice on how to sharpen her sales skills; she came to see me. She brought along her portfolio, and I asked her to role-play a little bit, to let me play the buyer and in this way walk me through her sales process. She agreed and immediately launched into a little memorized routine. Without bothering to connect with me in any meaningful way or get any sense of what my priorities were, she immediately opened up her portfolio and went into a long, boring, and extremely detailed description of each of the designs in her folder.

I was being as patient as I possibly could—she was, after all, quite well known in her field. When she got to the eighth design, though, I said, "Stop." Quizzically, she looked at me and asked what was wrong.

"Well," I said, "just suppose that the first seven designs you just described didn't work for me. Do you really think you would have had my attention by the time you got to the eighth design?"

She thought about that for a moment and then smiled sheepishly. She had made the classic sales mistake of believing that she was at the highest level of influence when *she* was doing the talking.

Actually, as sales leaders know, the opposite is actually true: The person speaking is generally at the *lowest* level of influence. Your level of influence rises only when the other person becomes engaged in the conversation and participates actively.

The Leader's Advantage

Even if customers are still looking at you as you speak, they are likely to shut down and stop listening when they decide you are trying to sell them.

If we are to have influence as salespeople and as leaders, we need two things from our prospects: their time and their attention.

When we start a one-on-one meeting with someone, the only thing we can be certain that we have is this person's time. We have no idea whether we've got his or her undivided attention. If we're doing all the talking, the other person could well be thinking about what else needs to be done today, what's going to be on the menu for lunch, or when this salesperson is going to shut up. If the prospect's mind is on other things while you're puking your features all over the place, how much of your message do you really think will get across? And why does the prospect need to hear about your features, anyway? These days, thanks to the Internet, customers could read all about your features online if they wanted to. *They don't need you to puke on them!*

I shared this lesson with the aforementioned fashion designer; she took it to heart and stopped puking everywhere. She started to meet her prospects, build up a little rapport, and find out what they were trying to accomplish in the market. Then she would review the one, two, or three designs that seemed most likely to produce the person's desired outcomes. She noticed a dramatic increase in interest for her designs, and she closed more business. She learned to do what sales leaders are supposed to do: help their customers get to the *promised land*—the place *they* want to go.

That's your job as a leader: connect with people and find ways to get them to the promised land. Your job is definitely *not* to puke all over potential customers; rather, it is to find out where the customer is trying to go. Identify the OUTCOME that makes the most sense for both of you, and then remove the obstacles in the way. Your job is to be creative and help customers find more efficient ways of doing things. Your job is to manage multiple constituencies and alliances, and to use those alliances to identify new and better ways of generating the desired results. Your job is to do what most salespeople *don't* do: *lead* the conversation with your prospects and customers about the results they need, the problems they have, and the obstacles they face. Solving these issues will lead them to promotions, increased business, higher profitability, higher productivity, enhanced competitive advantage, and a better quality of life.

The Job of Being a Sales Leader Never Ends

Leadership selling is not restricted to the selling process. You have to excel at getting people to the promised land throughout your entire relationship with them! Once you stop acting as a leader—once you stop trying to identify the interests of the customer and build alliances on behalf of those interests—you can rest assured that your base of business will start to evaporate.

> ### The Leader's Advantage
>
> In today's economy, salespeople have to prove their value with every sale. They cannot rely on loyalty from past transactions. The result is they have to have a positive impact on the careers and lives of everyone with whom they connect, every time. Otherwise, they may still have great relationships but only a fraction of the business they need and deserve.

You Sell Ideas

Like all effective leaders, top-producing salespeople sell ideas. They look for ways to find and improve the outcomes that their customers are seeking, and they start by talking about the "what." *What* are customers looking for?

As a leader, you must determine the "what" before the "how"—the "how" comes second. Your products and services represent the "how," which means that they are *not* what you should be starting the conversation with.

Read that again: *You should not start the conversation on your products and services*—even though you may have received vast amounts of technical training and even though you may know the "how" of your product and service like the back of your hand. If you start the conversation with the "how," you will leave out the most important part of the conversation, namely, the *outcomes* you are going to produce together.

These may sound like obvious points, but the sad truth is that salespeople ignore them routinely.

Beginning with the "how" guarantees that your conversation will be short and will produce little to no forward movement in the sales process. You may not even be given the opportunity to *discuss* the prospect's goals or the outcomes you hope to produce with him or her. Imagine how many sales meetings initiated by that fashion designer ended abruptly because of some sudden emergency that came up while she was soliloquizing about her many designs.

People tend to have very short attention spans these days. They have a lot on their mind, and the higher up they are on the food chain the less time they have for things that don't demonstrate immediate value to them. That's why we must prove in the first few seconds of a conversation that there is a reason someone should give us their undivided attention *and* their time.

Initiating a conversation by discussing the outcomes—as a leader does—makes all the difference when it comes to winning attention, winning time, closing more deals, expanding the size of the deal, and increasing margins. Launching the conversation in a different way allows you to lay the foundation for a value proposition that is second to none.

Lead with the Outcome!

Immediately focusing on the "how" limits your conversation with a potential customer strictly to features—features that most customers will think—correctly or incorrectly—that they have heard and seen elsewhere. There is little or no room there for differentiation! By leading with the outcome—as a true sales leader would—you can expand the conversation to other issues, issues that involve a larger piece of the pie. As the conversation expands, more and more opportunities will become available. These opportunities can lead to the sale of other goods and services.

For example, let's say that you are selling pool products to a homeowner who wants a new pump. You might be tempted to start talking about the features of your very best pool pump. Suppose you were to ask the homeowner what he or she would want from the new pump that the old pump didn't provide. The homeowner might think for a moment, then answer, "No downtime, better energy efficiency, and lower operating costs."

When you ask the potential customer to explain their reasons for wanting these features, you might hear a story of how the existing pump used to break down—typically on a hot summer day—and how the whole family would have to wait for the service rep to come and repair it. The use of the pool would be interrupted for days, and there would be a hefty repair bill to deal with.

Armed with this information, you can now talk about the *ideas and outcomes* that are most likely to make a difference to this buyer: Fewer breakdowns and lower bills! You could offer proof of your pump's energy efficiency and reliability, in the form of awards and articles praising its performance in these areas. You could then explain that your company offers a special extended warranty on the pump. This extended warranty is designed to reduce the risk of having downtime in the future, and it will also give the customer automatic top priority on service calls without costing a cent more on the repair bill.

You have just engaged your customer and secured his full, un-divided attention; every point you make is now landing with im-pact. You have just dramatically increased your chances of getting the deal, and you've done so by talking about the outcomes first. You may even have added to the size of the deal by introducing other products that support the outcomes that the customer is trying to attain.

At the end of the day, the customer is not buying a pump at all. The customer is actually buying uninterrupted pool time, reduced energy costs, and a lower cost of operation. *Those are outcomes!* This is exactly what Hayward Pool Products, the number one manufacturer of residential pool pumps, trains its dealers to do. And that, along with a great product, is why they are one of the leaders in their industry.

Why *Wouldn't* You Sell This Way?

For the past 20 years, I have been speaking to, advising, and coaching sales organizations of all sizes all around the world. Our clients have added at least half a billion dollars in incremental revenues by implementing this concept of leading with the outcome. In all of these situations, we never once changed the features of a company's product or service. We only changed the outcome.

You work for a company that already has a respectable product or service. If it didn't, you wouldn't be working there; the company would be out of business. The question, then, is a simple one: How do you communicate your value and differentiate yourself from the competition? The answer is just as simple: by selling like a leader does, by leading with the outcome.

Top-producing sales reps know that there is little competitive differentiation to be found in one's feature set. Those words may make marketing managers and technical departments cringe, but they nevertheless reflect the realities of the current market. Given today's astonishingly efficient information technology, the truth is that once you present a new feature, it will only take a short amount of time for the competition to find out what you're offering, reverse-engineer a competing offering, and start marketing their own version. How do you win that game?

The Leadership Mix

True differentiation from your competition comes by providing what I call the *leadership mix*. This is the unique mix of your features, services, quality, delivery, and leadership.

The Leader's Advantage

The leadership mix is what wins the game.

You need a different mix for each customer and each prospect. That means that no two sales you close as a leader are going to be alike, or even similar.

People buy for different reasons because they're seeking different *outcomes*. Our customers are looking to buy something that will support the unique *outcomes* that they are after. Leaders focus on the outcomes, and then they concentrate on the unique combination of features, services, quality, delivery, and coalition-building skills—the leadership mix—that will deliver the greatest value in achieving those outcomes. And that's not all! Leaders get people to experience those outcomes ahead of time, internally, before they actually occur. They use the leadership mix that they bring to any given situation as a tool—not simply for creating a single deal, but for establishing something much more important: a shared vision of the future.

The Leader's Wisdom

"The future has several names. For the weak, it is impossible. For the fainthearted, it is unknown. For the thoughtful and valiant, it is the ideal."—Victor Hugo

The mix you offer must become an offering in itself. Your sale can no longer revolve purely around features that people believe they can get elsewhere, or pricing that they believe they can beat by a tenth of a cent by shopping your bid around. The magic is in the mix!

Once you can do a better job of identifying a customer's desired outcomes, you can do a better job of creating the mix that will be perceived as most valuable in creating those outcomes—regardless of the dollar price that is connected to your offer. You can do a better job of persuading decision makers that even though they can get similar features from other sources, there is no other source that provides the same mix—the same comprehensive, multi-faceted plan for the future—that you do.

To create this kind of plan, you have to engage your prospects or customers in conversations about what is or could be possible—even when there is no short-term need for what you are selling. That's actually the best possible time to start making the sale! You'll discover why later on in the book. . . .

Your job is to align your *purpose* (outcomes) with the *vision* (outcomes) of the customer. Outcomes revolve around needs, fears, concerns, and desires. So that's what leaders talk about—not price or features!

Don't Waste Time!

Most salespeople usually don't sell from a position of leadership, and, as a result, end up wasting not only the customer's time, but their own precious time as well.

For instance, asking people what product or service they're using in a way that does not connect to any possible customer benefit is a waste of everyone's time. So is calling a potential customer and telling him that you will save him 10 percent, without even bothering to take the few minutes necessary to find out what's important to him. Reciting a particular product's list of features that your company drilled into you during product training—without having found any common ground with the prospect or customer—is a waste of everyone's time.

You can't expect to lead with any of these strategies because they don't connect to anything that's important in the customer's or prospect's world.

Leaders Don't Get Sidetracked by Price

People often don't buy the cheapest service or product available. Have *you* always purchased the cheapest alternative? No! You know you paid more for some items, based on certain issues and benefits that were more important to you—for whatever reason—than finding the item with the lowest price. When traveling by plane, some people pay extra for the benefits of first class; others don't. While some frequent flyers know they will have a good shot at upgrading to first class on a lower-fare ticket just before the scheduled flight time, others may pay the significantly higher fare simply to guarantee the first-class seat. It's that important to them. If you stop and think about it, you'll realize that there are lots of things in your own life that are far more important to you than getting the lowest possible price. For instance, buying name-brand products instead of generic brands, renting a high-priced apartment so you can have just the right view from your living room window, or buying expensive, front-row tickets to an NBA game.

"It All Sounds the Same!"

One of my mentors, the late Bill Brooks, was a well-known sales expert and coach to thousands of salespeople throughout the world. Bill once told me that he and a colleague conducted research on thousands of buyers across all industries and asked them this question: "Why do you beat salespeople up on price?"

In essence, the answer they got from buyers was this: "Put yourself in my shoes. I sit here at a desk, meeting with several salespeople daily, and they all do the same thing. They brag about all the bells and whistles they have to offer. But at the end of the day, it all sounds the same! When you feel that the offerings are more or less the same, you move to the next step and qualify them on price." For the sales leader, however, the discussion of price always comes at the end of the conversation—not the beginning! In fact, if the sales leader does the job right, pricing will be a secondary consideration when compared to other key factors in the buying decision.

Ask yourself this: What is the number one reason a purchasing manager would get fired? You may want to answer, "Paying too much for a product." Wrong! A purchasing agent's *first* responsibility is to keep the enterprise running efficiently and make sure it has the materials and services necessary to continue to supply its customers. If that supply chain is interrupted, the purchasing agent is out of a job. That's the top priority!

Once purchasing agents feel that they have multiple sources and a low risk of interrupting the supply chain, however, they move on to their next core responsibility: to drive cost out of the system. *If you appeal to that instinct, you will lose!* Instead, you must build a coalition that is based on the purchasing agent's primary responsibility, that which he or she shares with everyone else in the organization: keeping the enterprise running efficiently, so that it can satisfy customers.

When purchasing agents have access to multiple reliable suppliers, they will—if left to their own devices—put the squeeze on terms and conditions. To help offset this squeeze, you must lead by leveraging other relationships in the organization, relationships with people who can win by working with you, people who have a vested interest in the outcomes of your products and services. You must connect with the people whose careers depend on the results they produce, things like ease of use and zero-defect quality levels. These people must be in your "coalition of the winning!"

Your coalition might include the engineering manager, the production manager, the CIO, the CFO, the CEO—all of those players or someone else entirely. I don't much care what each person's title is. What I do care about is whether you are willing to do what leaders do—establish contacts at multiple levels in the organization.

The Leader's Advantage

If your coalition consists of a single person, you will lose.

Establishing multiple alliances and multiple points of contact is your best strategy for minimizing competitive pressures and bringing issues other than price to the forefront. This is what sales leaders do.

You Must Lead the Team

Traditionally, sales executives were the main point of contact with the customer. Years ago clients generally did not interact with other members of a selling organization. Today, however, customers will inevitably communicate with any number of people in our organization. The question is whether we as salespeople are going to be able to manage those points of contact.

Customer service and technical support are interacting with your customers in an effort to support their needs. Members of shipping and billing departments are also talking to your customers and attempting to ensure that they receive their products in a timely and professional manner. Even prospects you have not yet closed business with are just an e-mail message or a phone call away from your support team. Face it: Other people are in this game with you!

Sales executives today need to lead the efforts of their own internal support team, and must also coordinate support of the various contacts on the buyer's side. The salesperson must be prepared to emerge as team leader in a flexible network that not only crosses departmental lines, but also crosses the line between the selling and buying organizations! You must master not only the art of winning the deal, but also the art of winning buy-in, internally, on behalf of your customer.

Believe it: Your success as a salesperson depends on your ability to build and sustain coalitions both *inside* and *outside* your organization. You must create and lead the coalition, no matter what you are selling.

Many salespeople try to push back against this leadership message, but the message remains relevant all the same to a broad range of today's sales professionals. Even providers of professional services have to lead their internal support personnel. Your assistants and internal allies are all part of your team and, in a larger sense, your coalition. So, of course, are your prospects, customers, and clients.

OLD SALES MODEL

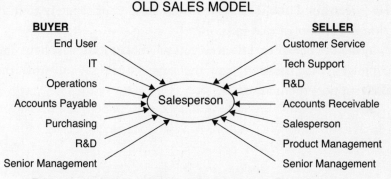

Every communication went through the salesperson. The salesperson was the connection and filter.

Figure 1.1

NEW SALES MODEL

Today, many points of contact from both sides interact with each other. The salesperson plays the role of the leader, facilitator, and quarterback.

Figure 1.2

The centers of influence both inside and outside your organization that refer new clients to you are also part of your team, your support network, and your coalition. *All of these people will only choose to become truly active and engaged members of your coalition if you make a conscious choice to take on a leadership role.*

All of these people are your critical business allies, and, today, your critical business allies must believe not only in your product or service features, but also in your mission and your capacity to inspire action in support of that mission.

In the next chapter, I'll show you what sales leaders believe about themselves, their mission, and the larger world...and how those beliefs support them as sellers.

2

The Five Beliefs of Effective Leaders

The leadership qualities that any sales executive must possess in order to produce exponentially profitable results are rooted in five powerful beliefs. Although, strictly speaking, it may not be *necessary* to build all five beliefs into your life, choosing to leave even one of these beliefs underdeveloped means missing out on opportunities and, ultimately, leaving money on the table.

Take a look now at the personal beliefs that will allow you to implement the seven essential traits of sales leadership.

Belief #1: You Have Everything You Need

You already have all the tools you need to make leadership selling a central reality of your life. Your job is simply to build on the qualities and resources that you already possess.

It doesn't matter what happened to you as a child. You are not missing anything. You can begin with what you have, and who you are, right here and right now. The sooner you accept this, the better

17

you will get to know the leader waiting within, and the faster and more enjoyable the process of adapting the seven sales leadership traits into your life will be.

Belief #2: You Can Improve *Any* Area of Your Life That You Choose

Every great leader in human history has found a way to use the process of self-discovery to expand his or her personal capacity and sense of self. I mention this because, if you are like most of the people I work with, you may be tempted, in a moment of weakness, to avoid developing one or more of the traits you'll be reading about in this book. This is a choice you might make based purely on a preconceived notion that a given trait "doesn't sound like you" or "doesn't feel like you."

I realize that some part of what you will encounter in this book may not sound like you *yet*. One or more elements on the list of leadership traits may not feel like you *yet*. You may not believe that you are that kind of person *yet*.

Here's my question: Do you *believe* that you are capable of improving yourself in any area of your life that you choose? If you feel that you have already grown as much as you can possibly grow—and learned as much as you can learn—then you may as well put this book away now, because it is not meant for you.

Great leaders are always more interested in what they *don't* yet know than in what they *do* know. They realize that any hope for future success can only come from learning and implementing *new* strategies. They believe they can improve themselves in any area of their lives that they choose. For these leaders, knowledge truly is power, because they are searching constantly for new knowledge that they can *apply* in their lives, and *applied* knowledge is what leads to success. If you wish to follow in the footsteps of the great sales leaders, you will need to make a personal commitment to learn and improve yourself in all of the areas we'll be discussing in this book.

Belief #3: Everything Is Possible

I challenge you, from this point forward, to approach everything that may seem to you to be uncomfortable, unfamiliar, or difficult with the highest possible level of open-mindedness. Truly successful people find ways to abandon biases that hold them back. *They believe great things are possible. They assume things CAN be done.*

There's a catch, of course. To achieve results that exceed what you are currently experiencing, you must change your actions.' To make great things possible, you must be willing to revise your strategies, your level of intensity, and your focus. After all, if what you're doing right now were generating the results you desired, you would already be where you wanted to be!

> ### The Leader's Advantage
>
> You must grow as a person, and be prepared to do things differently, if you wish to sell more.

In the pages that follow, I will also be challenging you to learn about some new selling strategies and to give them an honest try. You may well trip and fall while trying out these new strategies; in fact, you almost certainly will. It's extremely rare to succeed at any given venture the first time that it's attempted. But when you encounter difficulty, you will pick yourself up, dust yourself off, and start all over again—just as you did when you learned how to ride a bike.

You may wonder why you need to go through any of the discomfort or pain of changing; actually, you don't. You don't have to believe that whatever you want next in your life is possible. You don't have to grow. But you'll be happier in the long run if you do. Happiness *requires* growth, and growth inevitably involves pain. I've found that there are really two types of pain that are strongly associated with growth. It's important to be able to distinguish between the two.

The first kind of pain is the type that people generally try to avoid at all costs—that of arriving at a given point in life (for instance, the end of the fiscal year) and realizing that they have fallen short of a specific goal that they had set for themselves. That really *is* painful, since failing to meet a personal financial goal means that they did not support the goals and lifestyle that they had in mind for themselves!

The other kind of (more manageable) pain is one with which successful people deal regularly. It's the pain of trying something new and not really knowing how—or even *if*—it's going to work. This is the discomfort of unfamiliar effort, of figuring out what new steps you should be taking and then putting one foot in front of the other—even though it's a little unnerving to do so at first. This discomfort is similar to the minor aches and pains you get when you use muscles that haven't been used in a while; it's the pain of expanding your comfort zone. It's what you *should* be feeling on a daily basis.

The good news is that you get to decide which type of pain you will accept: the enduring pain of failure or the passing pain of change.

Sometimes, salespeople remain close-minded simply because they are afraid of trying new things. Open up your mind and assume the best. Allow yourself to venture forth into a new mindset and a new way of selling. *Start assuming that the best is possible!*

Belief #4: Preparation Maximizes Your Potential

To accept this belief, you must we willing to invest the time and effort necessary to do a better job of preparing yourself than the competition does. Having studied high achievers in all walks of life, I can assure you that all of them believe that preparation is an essential prerequisite to success.

The Leader's Wisdom

"Optimism is a strategy for making a better future. Because unless you believe that the future can be better, it's unlikely you will step up and take responsibility for making it so. If you assume that there's no hope, you guarantee that there will be no hope. If you assume that there is an instinct for freedom, that there are opportunities to change things, there is a chance you may contribute to making a better world. The choice is yours."—Noam Chomsky

A few years ago, I was working with Bud Howard, the then vice president of sales for Hertz Equipment Rental. Bud asked me the following question: "Ron, which do you think is most important: the will to win or the will to prepare?" I told him that I believed the will to prepare was far more critical to an individual's success. You may want to win, but if you don't do what is *necessary* to win, it will never happen. Both of us were on the same page; we both knew that preparation is the key to success in life.

This belief applies to almost any aspect of one's personal or professional life. It is especially obvious in the world of sports. As a lifetime Yankees fan and a long-term season ticket holder, I've been privileged to see some of the most gifted and exciting baseball players of the past 30 years. There have been a lot of great players over the years who have worn the pinstripes, including the Yankee that long-term fans are most likely to idolize: Mickey Mantle. This Hall of Famer was truly a phenomenal player; as a kid, I used to get excited every time Number Seven came up to bat. Watching him hit those trademark mammoth home runs is something I will never forget. And of course, Mantle did become one of the leading home run hitters in baseball history. Yet when I think about Mickey Mantle today, I do so with a feeling of melancholy; I can't escape the conclusion that Mickey Mantle never lived up to his true potential.

Yes, he was unlucky; he tripped in center field in the 1951 World Series and sustained a serious injury to his leg. But he had God-given talent on a baseball field—the kind that most mortals can only dream about. His strength, his ability to hit home runs of extraordinary dimensions, his speed—all of these things were off the charts. One in 10,000 major league prospects have Mantle's kind of ability.

Unfortunately, that extraordinary level of talent provided Mantle with an excuse to avoid preparation. Since he could outperform most of his opponents without much of an effort, he rarely made any. So the stories go, all too often his method of preparation consisted of a long night out partying and drinking and arriving at the ballpark just in time for the game.

The Leader's Wisdom

"Don't be like me," he said, addressing himself especially to children. "God gave me a body and the ability to play baseball. I had everything and I just . . ."

—Mickey Mantle in a press conference after his liver transplant, as quoted in The New York Times, July 12, 1995.

Now, consider another player in pinstripes—Don Mattingly—as an example of a completely different approach to the game. As a young prospect, Mattingly was someone whom most major league scouts would have assessed as having only average talent. He wasn't born with great baseball potential, and he didn't inspire the comparisons with legends like Babe Ruth or Jimmie Foxx during his rookie year in the majors that Mickey Mantle did. In fact, Mattingly had to work hard in his early years to make the very most of his potential if he hoped to make it to the big leagues. Instead of taking his ability for granted, he made every effort to improve and expand on the talents that he was fortunate enough to possess.

In reality, most of us are Don Mattinglys—not Mickey Mantles. Despite the fact that Mantle set more records and had more impressive numbers, Mattingly managed to get more from his skills than Mantle did; he had a better work ethic and did a much better job preparing for a game. He was more invested in the process of expanding his talent, and he was less likely to coast.

As someone who saw both men play, the skill that each displayed was incredibly impressive; but skill will only get you so far. Before every game, Don Mattingly would take a tee and hone his batting skills by hitting the ball into the net behind home plate. He did this every day, no matter how hot or tired he was—even when he was hitting well over .300 on the season. He knew that daily preparation was the reason he was hitting so well. I never saw Mantle do that on a regular basis, and I doubt that anyone else did.

Imagine what Mickey Mantle could have achieved if he prepared as well as Don Mattingly. It seems possible that Mantle could have been the first to break Babe Ruth's career home run record—and perhaps even extended his own career. I run into a lot of Mickey Mantle types in the organizations I work with. When I meet a high achiever who has not yet learned the value of getting the most out of his or her talents, I feel like giving the person a Don Mattingly baseball card and telling him or her to take a cue from this professional preparer!

Top producers need to do more of what Don Mattingly did—practice. They need to hone their skills in order to achieve their true potential in terms of creating revenue, and they also need to practice to help the other members of their team. Their true value lies not just in the hard numbers they generate, but also in their ability to mentor others and enhance the skills of the team as a whole. That is true sales leadership.

A truly positive outcome depends on the whole package: skills, mindset, and preparation. I have known senior executives whose organization was better off once they fired these top producers. Although these executives might have experienced short-term setbacks as a result of the lost business, they felt that they would lose more in the long run as a result of actions and attitudes from the superstar that negatively affected the team as a whole. Time after time, I have witnessed the wisdom of such decisions pay off for companies.

Which kind of superstar do *you* want to be? Whether you are a Mickey Mantle with born talent or a Don Mattingly who's had to practice relentlessly and develop a fierce work ethic to deliver MVP results, my message to you is simple: You shouldn't put off practice and wait until you are in the batter's box, facing your first pitch of a real, live game to begin to develop your skills. Practice must happen—and happen often—*before* the game.

The Leader's Advantage

Of course, when you practice, you must make sure you are practicing the right things. Practicing the wrong things for the sake of practice is deadlier than not practicing at all.

When the clock starts ticking, and you are in front of the client, it is game time! Are you truly prepared for the one—and possibly only—chance you may have with this person?

Here's another reason to practice. If you are not willing to sell yourself on change, then how can you convince your prospects and customers to do the same? *That* is what you are really selling: change. Not quality, not service, not increased market share—change. Think about it; if you want to push through a price increase, you are asking the customer to change, specifically to change his or her perception of how much they're willing to pay for the value you have to offer. If you are looking to sell more to an existing customer, you are asking that customer to change his or her perception as to how much business you truly deserve. If you want the prospect to change vendors and buy from you, you are asking the prospect to change an existing set of procedures and routines to something that you believe will work better.

In order to get someone else to be willing to go outside of their comfort zone, you must exhibit the behavior first and make a habit out of getting out of your comfort zone in your own life! People will follow your lead if they sense that you are the kind of person who routinely prepares for and implements positive change in your own life. But if you can't show that you're that kind of person, people will be hesitant to follow you. You must move first. If you want to change the quality of the conversations you're having with your prospects and customers, you need to change the conversation you are having with yourself first.

Belief #5: Customers Come First

Why does a focus on customers matter? Because no revenues or profits are gained—until a sale is made. Whether you are the owner of a company, a key executive, a sales representative, or a provider of professional services, your money is not truly earned until someone buys something.

Now, let's suppose that you're having a tough quarter and have fallen behind on some hefty bills. You're on your way to meet with a prospect who could ensure, beyond a shadow of a doubt, that you will exceed quota this year—and allow you to pay all of your bills and then some. As you drive to the meeting, would you be thinking more about closing the deal . . . or about the needs of that prospect?

Real sales leaders adopt a *completely* customer-focused mindset. They internalize the same things customers internalize, worry about the same things customers worry about, and generally experience the same emotions their customers experience. Sales leaders live by this commandment: Nothing gets sold if customers don't feel like their issues, needs, wants, and desires have been fulfilled. It's not about you; it's about them.

The Leader's Wisdom

"A leader needs two things—a goal and to meet the needs of others."—Dr. Edward A. Ciccoricco

---

Good leaders do two things: They set goals that others can buy into, and they make sure that others' needs are met. Your own personal goal, on its own, is not enough to inspire another person! Your goal may be closing the deal, but if your customer has concluded that his or her core needs are not met by this relationship, then there will be no sale. There needs to be a mutual understanding, a connection that satisfies the needs of both parties.

During the 9/11 attacks, all U.S. aircrafts were grounded and the skies were closed for several days. Jumbo planes coming to the United States from Europe were diverted to Eastern Canada, and forced to land in communities where the number of local citizens was far outnumbered by the number of people on the planes.

Many of these townspeople only possessed the bare necessities. The unusual situation ended up revealing a lot about the values of the community. A police officer in Newfoundland was asked, "How did you deal with this disaster with little or no supplies?" He answered that no one had to be told what to do; the people in those towns simply donated whatever they had to the travelers in need. Some even shared towels when they only had one towel per family member to begin with. The police officer described the generosity as "a spontaneous combustion of caring." What a powerful phrase! Suddenly, people were looking out for each other. Suddenly, people who had been strangers to one another had powerful bonds connecting them.

What you can take away from that story is this: People tend to follow others when they feel that "spontaneous combustion of caring." Leaders know this fundamental truth well. Influence and power only come from another person's feeling that their basic needs, wants, and desires are being met. Your customers truly don't care about your mortgage payments or career burdens. They want to know how you are going to make a difference in *their* lives. If they feel you are only out for yourself, you may still get the deal, but you will likely be missing out on all the potential business that is available. Dollars will be left on the table. Your prospects and customers need to see, touch, and feel that "spontaneous combustion of caring." Don't worry. When people genuinely have that feeling, you will get more from them than you ever dreamed possible.

Are You Ready?

If you're willing to accept these five core beliefs, you're ready for leadership. You're ready to start studying—and implementing—the seven traits of great sellers.

Read on.

3 | The Seven Traits of Great Sellers

I wish I had the opportunity to offer a personal word of thanks to each and every one of the sales leaders I've worked with over the years. These are the people who inspired the list of traits I'm summarizing briefly in this chapter, and expanding upon in the later chapters of this book. There have been thousands of leaders in my life, and I've learned so much from them that it took me years to identify the most important traits they all shared. If you're one of them, and you happen to be reading this book, you know who you are. Consider this chapter my "thank-you" message to you, and the rest of the book my attempt to pass along, and live up to, your example.

Here, without further ado, are the seven traits that the truly great salespeople I've worked with all had in common.

Trait #1: Visualizing

Let's think about the word "visionary." It connotes the ability to perceive an outcome *before* it takes physical form—an ability to look to the future, to ask big questions, and set substantial goals. Leaders know how to visualize it (whatever "it" may be at any given moment);

29

they have a plan for their organization. In the same way, top producing sales representatives have a vision for the success of their clients and themselves.

The problem is that most people don't "visualize it." They check off items on a to-do list—usually, someone else's to-do list. They go through the day with a task orientation and never enter into a purpose orientation.

Your vision is your purpose. It should drive all of your actions. As a sales executive, your vision—and everything involved in it—must determine your actions on a daily basis. It must serve as the basis of all your conversations. So, ask yourself this: What is your vision? What is your purpose? You must become clear about your own purpose in life.

Leaders start with the end in mind. They visualize where they are going *first,* and then they operate from there. They don't make a long list of all their past experiences and use those as their guide to what should happen next. They learn from past experience, of course, but they are not prisoners of their experience. While events from your past may have been fruitful, they can also cloud your judgment of what can truly be achieved. Leaders know that visualizing their desired outcome is the essential first step to breaking down barriers to success. Then, they work backward in figuring out the actions required to achieve the end goal. They don't operate as they have in the past; they simply use selected methods that have worked before as tools for creating a new future. They use a clean slate to create the future they desire from scratch.

What is your vision? What outcome are you willing to think about and visualize? Whether it is supporting a certain lifestyle, ending a certain disease, or acting on behalf of some other worthy cause, you must be clear of the outcomes you want to produce in your life, and you must be willing to visualize them. If you cannot visualize your desired outcomes, then you are lacking the vision of a leader.

It's extremely important to work toward goals that resonate with your passions and interests. Some people tend to choose goals that do not really connect strongly to a personal vision; they are deciding upon a goal simply for the sake of having one.

This may be difficult advice to follow, but it's important: Don't get distracted by money. Money, in and of itself, is not your vision. It is what the money will provide for you that imparts the motivating factor. You must visualize something that is going to drive you to the end and act as a magnet; so that when the forces of life come your way and throw you off the tracks, it will be easy for you to be pulled back on track, and keep moving toward your destination.

A CEO with whom I've worked for a long time poses an interesting interview question to every salesperson she considers hiring: "Tell me what you are personally committed to achieving in your life within the next 24 months." She's trying to find out whether the person she's talking to has a vision. The answer she gets tells her a lot about the person she's interviewing. If a potential colleague simply can't answer the question, then she knows she is not dealing with someone for whom vision is an important part of life. On the other hand, if the person instantly starts talking with energy and articulates a clear goal—one that can be visualized—she knows she's dealing with someone who has a vision and who would make an excellent addition to her team.

How would *you* answer her? Would you be able to? Do you have a vision?

Nobody can provide you with the vision necessary to motivate you. But once you have it—and the drive to make it happen—others can create the environment to help you reach your true potential.

Leaders know their own vision, and they are, by the same token, endlessly curious about the goals of others. Too many salespeople are so concerned with making the sale that they act solely on a task-focused basis; they go straight for the close, puking along the way, and learning nothing whatsoever about the people to whom they're trying to sell. They spill their guts as to what their products can do, and even why and how they are going to make a difference in the customers' lives, all without asking their customers one meaningful question about what *their* vision is or what outcomes they are trying to generate. Before you start puking, find out what they are envisioning! Find out how the customer's desired outcomes can align with your vision. You cannot sell value without entering into this process.

Trait #2: Positioning

You've just learned that sales leaders are purpose driven, not task driven. That means their focus is on end results. They work on purpose, and they begin doing so from the very earliest moments of the sales process. They know how important those early moments are, and they are purposeful when it comes to the very first impressions they leave with people. In other words, they know how to position themselves.

Solid positioning lays the foundation for the entire relationship to come, and it allows sales leaders to make the choices about how to move forward in the sales cycle that make the most strategic sense.

Most salespeople are too busy jumping through hoops to spend a lot of time thinking about positioning. They don't give a lot of conscious thought to the first impression they intend to leave. Sales leaders, on the other hand, position themselves powerfully in the minds of their customers as uniquely qualified resources who are capable of adopting a totally customer-focused mindset.

Determining the first impression they want to leave, and then leaving that impression and no other impression, is a big part of what sales leaders do for a living. They know that the way they position themselves at the beginning of the relationship has a profound impact on where they end up—how fast they're able to close the deal—how much they're able to get for the deal—and who they have access to along the way.

This book will show you exactly what you need to do to position yourself strategically, as a leader, at the beginning of every sales process you undertake.

Trait #3: Building Alliances

Building new relationships and alliances, and strengthening existing ones, is a major part of the leader's job description. In fact, this is what leaders spend most of their time doing. They use relationships to accomplish their critical goals—and that means building bridges on a regular basis.

> ### The Leader's Advantage
>
> Leaders reach out for a living!

The alliances that leaders form make it possible for them to leverage their personal influence exponentially, both in their own organizations and within the organizations of the people with whom they're working. Truly great salespeople leverage their influence in exactly the same way so they can build constituencies on both the selling side and the buying side.

It never ceases to amaze me how often I run into salespeople who don't much like building new alliances. They have eight or ten people whom they call on a regular basis, and they're pretty comfortable dealing with those same people over and over again. Typically, these people operate only at one level in the organization, and refuse to initiate contact at other levels. These are the salespeople who avoid finding new centers of influence, and potential contacts that could become their next qualified lead in a given company. These people are not sales leaders.

If you are looking to increase sales, you need to make contact with new people on a daily basis. You must constantly reach out to create new alliances with new people—alliances that align with your vision, alliances that harness the power of two or more minds to produce results that no member in the alliance could have produced individually. This is the concept behind every good team. When two or more people come together with their ideas and start to dialogue, solutions develop that would *not* have been created had it not been for the combination of ideas. For the same reason, you must also stay in contact with your base of existing contacts. You need to constantly widen your circle to attract a bigger piece of the pie and create better outcomes for everyone. This book shows you how to build powerful alliances and significantly expand your sphere of influence.

Trait #4: Asking Good Questions

Good questions are, inevitably, big-picture questions—questions that connect your vision to the prospect's world.

If, for example, you are a financial advisor, and your vision is to help your clients live the life they desire, then your first question should not be, "What are you currently investing in?" That kind of question won't win attention or time. The big-picture question that you want to ask will sound like this: "What are the three things you want your money to provide for you in the future?" or "Can you describe for me the ideal lifestyle you want to live—now and in the future?"

The scope of the question determines the level of success that a sales leader is likely to attain. Of course, I am talking here about the *value* the question points toward. Great leaders use big questions to establish themselves as potential resources for their allies and to highlight the difference between where someone is and where that person is trying to go. They know that using questions to determine their allies' desired destination is the key to identifying new opportunities. The more that a salesperson uncovers dissatisfaction with the status quo—through "issues questions," which you'll be learning more about later on in this book—the greater the zone of opportunity you will identify, and the more credibility you will establish as a leader in the relationship.

Leaders know that with the questions they ask they can control not merely patterns of conversation, but patterns of *thought* as well. They realize that the art of uncovering opportunities lies in analyzing—and acting on—the answers to their big questions. They know that clients and prospects will immediately judge the potential value of a salesperson by the conversations they initiate and the questions they pose. These questions determine your success in getting the deal, and perhaps more important, they determine how big the deal will be and how much residual income it will produce for you over time.

Power and influence come not from the statements you make or the claims you put forward, but from the answers you receive to the big questions you pose.

If you listen to the quality of the questions someone asks, you will instantly be able to tell whether he or she is task oriented or outcome oriented. A person who poses thought-provoking questions will always secure your time and attention—like Tim Russert, the long-time host of NBC's news interview program *Meet the Press,* who in 2008 passed away suddenly at age 58. His passing was a significant loss for many, including the people he made uncomfortable during interviews by posing tough questions. Tim made a career out of asking powerful questions. They may not have been the easiest ones to answer, but they provided the greatest insights into incredibly important issues, events, and people.

Do you want to learn how to ask such questions—powerful questions that will attract allies, lead you to exactly the information you need, and boost your career? Then, by all means, read on!

Trait #5: Creating Powerful Value Propositions

Your *value proposition* is the tool customers use to decide whether or not you are going to get the deal. The simple formula for the value proposition is:

$$CNC - CC = PV$$

- CNC stands for Cost of No Change—that is, the cost of not accepting your proposal.
- CC stands for Cost of Change. This cost is defined in terms of the time, money, and effort it takes to acquire, learn about, and use your service.
- PV stands for Perceived Value.

The basic rule of thumb is that in order to acquire perceived value, the cost of no change (that is, the consequence of not accepting your proposal) has to be greater than the perceived costs of buying from you. For example, let's suppose your average sale is $30, and let's say that you believe purchasing my book will help you close exactly one extra sale. The cost of no change (in other words, the loss of the potential $30 sale) therefore outweighs the cost of this book ($24.95).

Perceived Value Equation Example: CNC ($30) − CC ($24.95) = PV ($5.05)

So you figure that there is a value of $5.05. Now let me ask you this: Is $5 really enough to prompt you to go online and order the book or to drive to the bookstore? Probably not! But what if I were to convince you that by reading my book you would increases your sales, not by $30, but by, say, $200,000? Now, the equation reads CNC (loss of $200k in extra sales) minus the cost of the book and effort of acquisition ($24.95 + effort). The perceived value stands at a gain of roughly $199,975. Would you run to the bookstore or log on to an online store for $199,975?

Perceived Value Equation Example: CNC ($200k) − CC ($24.95) = PV ($199,975)

Maybe your answer was "yes." But the reality is some people might *not* take action for that amount of money! If you're a top producer making $4 million a year, a gain of $199,975 actually may not be enough to inspire you to take action. You may need to see a figure of $500,000 or more before you start paying attention!

The point is people are only moved to action if there is enough of an incentive for them to do so. Of course, the right incentive is not always measured in dollars. It is the sum total of all types of measures people use to determine value. This book provides all the information you need on how to create and deliver powerful value propositions, based on both tangible and intangible incentives that motivate buyers to take action.

Trait #6: Communicate Persuasively

The best leaders communicate persuasively and inspire action in others. To put it bluntly, their message is more than the sum of its parts. They deliver their points with eloquence and style that is congruent—not just with the details of what they are saying—but with their larger purpose. When you communicate with congruence, you express a level of authenticity that immediately and positively impacts the people you are trying to serve—and makes *them* eager to connect with and serve you. People who cannot communicate with purpose and congruence seldom win many allies—and never make effective leaders.

Once, after I had given a speech in Chicago, the management team of the company that had hired me invited me out to dinner. During the walk back from the restaurant to the hotel, the vice president of marketing was complaining that she had written the best memo of her life to her sales people, but no one read it or acted upon it. I suggested that maybe it wasn't the best memo of her life. Don't get me wrong—the memo probably had killer content and ideas, but if no one read it or did anything with the information that was in it, guess what? It was not as valuable as she thought it was!

The same holds true for sales presentations. Salespeople spend so much time on developing killer presentations that have all the bells and whistles that they tend to ignore the essential question of how they will need to *deliver* the presentation for maximum impact. After all, what is your ultimate goal: creating artful presentations or closing sales?

A client of mine once did a needs analysis for a prospect, and developed a phenomenal PowerPoint on his findings. He spent two whole days developing an elaborate presentation complete with graphics, video, and lots of catchy typefaces. He went in the following week and gave the presentation. At the end, he asked how he had done. The answer: "You were phenomenal, but didn't you hear?

We re-organized last week, and everything has changed. What you covered in the presentation really isn't that relevant anymore."

An effective sales leader would have started that conversation by asking, "Has anything changed since we last met?" That question would have looked past the details of the presentation and tied the discussion to the larger *purpose* of the meeting.

Things change daily—not just in your world, but also in your customer's world. You must communicate persuasively if you wish to be part of that change. You can get all the facts "right"—and still be hopelessly behind the curve when it comes time to inspire action. You can't research your way to persuasiveness, nor can flashy words and graphics close the gap for you. You must look closely at your strategies, your timing, your rapport with the audience, and your delivery style. In this part of the book, I'll show you the simple but incredibly effective strategies sales leaders use to energize their presentations and close more and bigger deals.

Trait #7: Holding Yourself Accountable

The best leaders assume accountability for their outcomes. They are personally responsible for their own world and to the allies they attract. They never hide behind the organization, and they never make excuses—to themselves or anyone else.

CEOs sometimes tell me how frustrated they are with their employees not being accountable to the organization. I always answer that there is no such thing as accountability to an organization; rather it is *personal* accountability that matters. People are accountable to other people—not organizations. In fact, it all starts with responsibility to yourself. How in the world can you expect to keep commitments to others if you don't first keep commitments to yourself?

Leaders make promises to themselves first, and then follow through on those promises. It's their dedication to their own vision and standards that make it possible for them to follow through when they make commitments to other people. This book gives you the tools you need to make—and follow through on—the critical commitments you must make to *yourself* as you build all seven of these traits into your career and your life. Here, you will take the action steps that make this book an ongoing resource in your life, not just a placeholder on your bookshelf.

If you follow the program, then you will join the elite few who make personal commitments and personally deliver on those commitments. The rewards you will reap will astonish you. In the final analysis, your *journey to sales leadership* starts and ends with your own personal accountability.

Are you ready to begin that journey?

4 | Visualizing

They say that if you don't know where you're going all roads will get you there. In sales, you have a choice of two roads. The first is the wide road, the road of stiff competition, where everyone is vying about price or the same two or three familiar issues. There are a lot of people traveling on that road—in fact, it's awfully crowded. On the other hand, you can also choose the narrower road—that of competitive advantage. This is where you differentiate yourself in a dramatic way from the competition by proving that you're operating on an entirely distinct level, addressing issues that you and you alone have raised with this prospect. This road is downright lonely, which is just the way you want it. If you choose the road less traveled—to paraphrase Robert Frost—that really *will* make all the difference.

The road you travel will be determined by your ability to visualize. When I talk about "vision," I mean the ability to create mental pictures that describe the long-term outcomes you plan to build for yourself, your organization, and your customer.

Visualize Big!

Picture this: You are the CEO of a technically savvy company that creates breakthrough products, chemical reagents that significantly

41

cut the cost of processing metals. You bring the new technology to market without competition, and sales soar.

Eventually, your competitors figure out that there is money to be made in the market you've just created, and they develop and offer a similar product. A few years pass, and you realize that your world market share isn't what it once was. The "wallet share" of your largest customer's volume of this product drops significantly. Now what do you do?

This was the dilemma that the mining division of a major chemical company found themselves facing when they contacted me in 1992. After I gave a talk for their division, the vice president and key account manager brought me out to their office to take part in a strategy meeting. The contracts at their single biggest customer were expiring, and they were supposed to submit a bid for the entire account when I became involved.

Upon arriving at our meeting, I looked at my new clients and asked them this question: "What do you want to achieve with this customer as a result of my intervention?" They immediately answered, "We want to win the bid."

I pushed them a little bit. "Is that really what you want to *achieve* with this customer? Imagine you had a blank piece of paper and you could create your own destiny just by writing words on that sheet. What do really want to *achieve* with this customer?" When they realized what I was asking, they quickly became more passionate and engaged. Suddenly they were asking questions like, "Why do we have to bid at all?" After all, they'd created this technology; in their minds what they had to offer was technically superior to anything that *any* competitor had to offer.

I took their responses to this and went even further by asking, "Okay, you want to negotiate an agreement as opposed to having to bid for the business. What percentage of their business do you want? You now have 25 percent of the account." They answered, of course, "We want 50 percent."

I responded, "Fifty percent? Remember, you're creating your destiny. What do you *really* want?"

After a glance between the two of them, the answer came back: "We want 75 percent of the business."

"For how long?" I asked.

"Ten years," they answered.

Now they had the vision. They knew exactly what they wanted to achieve with this customer in terms of specific numbers and time parameters. They didn't know *how* they were going to achieve it—yet. We figured that part out together; but I knew we couldn't start doing that until the vision had been established.

Over the following 18 months, we took the lead and designed a process that completely transformed that company's relationship with its customer ... a process that led to a negotiated 10-year supply agreement for 75 percent of the customer's demand. No bid was ever submitted. Everything that chemical company accomplished with its customer started with their vision—a clear sense of what management wanted to make happen.

Reinventing the Business

In 2003, when I began my work with the president and owner of Timber Trading, Tim Seale, Tim had built a successful wholesale lumber business over a period of decades. However, he was beginning to realize that there was only going to be a certain premium that customers would pay to a middleman to facilitate deals between the lumber yards and mills. He recognized that the only way he would remain profitable in the future was to add value to the process. I was privileged to be part of the team that helped Timber Trading develop the vision that allowed them to do exactly that.

Tim decided to buy the lumber and bring it to a warehouse where he could regrade it and create a product that far exceeded industry-acceptable standards. His company created a whole new packaging and labeling system that actually drove down inventory costs for lumberyards. He added a few more innovative products and services along the way, until one day his competitors looked up and realized that Tim had just created a whole new way of doing business.

Tim Seale was—and is—a visionary. He knew that if he wanted to position his company for success, the wholesale model of the past was not going to work. He had to rethink what it meant to be a value-add wholesaler, someone whose value was worth having and paying for. He realized that a new vision was in order and that a whole new set of actions were required if he was to succeed in turning that vision into reality.

Tim had to re-educate his salespeople on how to think and sell; the salespeople in turn had to influence a whole market about why it made sound strategic sense to change the existing method of procuring lumber. This process of change was not instantaneous. It took time and a lot of work, and some of the transitions were challenging. Customers did not come along for the ride that easily in the beginning; in fact, some did not come along at all. Tim had to clarify what type of customer he really wanted to attract in order for his new model to work. Not everyone with whom he had been doing business previously was a viable candidate.

Every time frustration hit, Tim and his people found a way to work through it. It would have been easy for them to quit. But Tim's clarity of vision, along with his passion and commitment, drove his company's transformation. In speaking with Tim recently, I asked him to recall the other factors that had made the transition possible. He said, "In moments of doubt, it's important to surround yourself with advisers who reinforce the vision, who support you. This is not meant to sound too solicitous, Ron, but I believe that this is the role that you played for me in the visioning and implementation process that we went through at Timber Trading."

At the end of the day, Timber Trading survived the housing downturn that crippled the building industry and the lumber industry in particular. They made it through because they understood the importance of visualizing the future and building a plan based on that future.

How to Create a Clear Vision

Creating a clear vision definitely does *not* mean that you have all of the answers figured out ahead of time. When I started out with the aforementioned chemical company, we did not know exactly *how* we were going to win 75 percent of that critical customer's business for the next 10 years. Similarly, when Tim Seale began to redefine his business model, he did not know about every hurdle that he was going to encounter along the way, and he certainly didn't know how he was going to respond to those hurdles.

You don't need all the answers up front; in fact, if you have all the answers right away, then that's a sign that you haven't yet established a clear vision! Any effective vision requires that you pose some questions to which you don't know the answers. Did John F. Kennedy have all the answers about how the U.S. space program was going to place a man on the moon when he challenged the country to accomplish this feat?

The Leader's Wisdom

We need men who can dream of things that never were.
—John F. Kennedy

A clear vision is one that asks questions that haven't yet been answered. And to create one, you need the end in sight first. Then you can backtrack and figure out the answers; that's a matter of implementation.

Yes, of course you need a good plan to connect up with your vision. But the real results come from the compelling vision you set for yourself up front, followed by your ongoing analysis and modifications along the way. There are always unforeseen obstacles that need to be dealt with. If you try to create a vision for yourself or your prospect that supplies solutions for all obstacles ahead of time, you are not engaged in leadership selling but in some abstract version of troubleshooting. There's a time and a place for troubleshooting, of course . . . but it's not vision.

Start with a clear vision, the clear plan will come later!

Seven Elements of a Clear Vision

Here are seven great tools you can use to create a unique vision for yourself and for your prospect.

1. **Start with a Blank Piece of Paper.** Do not construct your vision on what you think is possible based on your past experiences. Think about the life you want to live, the level you want to reach in your business or career, the competitive threats you want to overcome now, and how you want to overcome them. Think about what it will take for you to reach and sustain your goals. Proceed on the assumption that anything is possible.

2. **Apply the "Think Tank" Method.** This is group brainstorming. It's a great way to create a vision that is not biased by past experiences. Initially, the chemical company thought that getting their customer to agree to a long-term negotiated agreement at substantially higher volumes was impossible. If we hadn't assembled a think tank and explored some unconventional ideas as a group, we never would have found a way to

produce the outcome that we did. It takes discipline to fight off old thoughts of what is possible in any given situation; sometimes it takes interaction with another person or a group of people. A solid, compelling vision must push through all discomfort, habit, and complacency. Convening a think tank is a great way to start this process. Put whatever comes to mind down on paper, no matter how ridiculous it sounds. Do not try to rationalize whether or not a given idea will work. Get it all down. Just brainstorm, then evaluate it all as a group later.

3. **Make It Specific.** Following a vision that has no specific details is like trying to hit a bull's-eye in the dark. "Increasing my sales this year" is not a vision. After all, an increase of sales by a single dollar would meet the challenge you've set. If you're looking to buy that luxurious second home on the beach, you will need a lot more than an extra dollar in sales revenues for you to attain that goal. A vision should answer these questions: What, specifically, are we trying to make happen? What are you (and your prospect) willing to work for, to fight to make happen? Why? How will you know when it has happened? How will you know when you're halfway there? Or a quarter of the way? If you can't measure your progress towards the fulfillment of the vision, then it's not specific enough!

4. **Make Sure Your Vision Is Something You Can Evangelize.** Guy Kawasaki, author of *Selling the Dream,* reminds his audiences about how evangelistic selling is required for anyone who is committed to carrying out a vision. One of Kawasaki's favorite examples involves the early days of Apple Computer, when the company's founders were building computers in a garage. Kawasaki also recalls launching systems into the market when doing so required software companies to buy into the dream and develop applications for a platform that did not yet exist.

Guy sees evangelism as something that uses a *cause* as the embodiment of a vision. He identifies the four building blocks of evangelism as follows: leaders, angels, evangelists, and enemies. You need all four. (Notice how the first building block mentioned involves leadership.) Tim Seale had to be an evangelist to bring about the changes he envisioned. So did the managers at the chemical company I discussed in the beginning of the chapter, and so did the teams at both that chemical company and Timber Trading. They all had to sell the dream, evangelize, and create a new way of doing things based on their own belief in their goals, dreams and commitments. They also had to be willing to face the inevitable pain of change on a personal level. First and foremost, though, they had to have a leader who saw the cause clearly.

During a conversation with Steve Forbes, CEO of Forbes Inc., I had the chance to ask him about his Internet strategy. He said, "We made the Internet a strategic priority starting in 1996. Our sites now attract 20 million unique visitors every month. This has helped increase revenues from advertising." That was visionary thinking, and a great example of evangelistic leadership. Unlike other publishers who simply put their magazine and newspaper content online, Forbes set up an entirely distinct organization that was physically separate from the magazine. Today, 98 percent of Forbes.com's content is non-Forbes magazine material. Did you have that kind of dedicated web site in 1996? Did you even *have* a web site in 1996? This kind of foresight is one of the values that make Steve Forbes a speaker in demand when it comes to anticipating the trends and demands of the future economy.

To be an effective evangelist:
- You must have courage and be willing to take risks when answers and success are not guaranteed. Remember: There

was no guarantee supporting Forbes' venture onto the Internet!

■ You must be willing to pick yourself up and dust yourself off when things don't work out as you had planned. You have to be ready to learn from your mistakes and change what's not moving you forward toward the fulfillment of your dream. Notice that this is *not* the same thing as changing your dream altogether! Sales leaders know how to make small tweaks along the way.

■ You must lead the way with new actions and behaviors, even when customers and others are initially skeptical. You cannot let the doubts and negativity of other people stop you. If someone's negative attitude is enough to derail your vision for yourself or your prospect, you are not a sales leader—or any other kind of—leader.

> ### The Leader's Wisdom
>
> "The strength of belief must be a greater force than the opposition of doubt!"—Tim Seale, owner of Timber Trading

5. **Use Intuitive Judgment in Support of Your Vision.** Creating a new vision and starting a new conversation about that vision requires intuitive judgment. You may not have historical data to fall back on that guarantees the results you want. Many visionaries lack such data! If your intuition tells you that what you are doing is the right thing to do, though, you must build a plan around that intuition. Listen to your own voice. Then start communicating what you are planning, and why, to the right people.

A friend of mine, the great entrepreneur Al Parinello, once told me that he often came up with the answers to his most pressing problems of the day during the brief moments when he was falling asleep or awakening from the previous night's sleep—the times of day when he was going into or coming out of an unconscious state. Al said, "You must think about a present challenge *before* retiring for the evening for this process to work. The conscious mind can only communicate with the latent mind in those few seconds before falling asleep and before awakening. If this is done properly, the right answers will sometimes snap into your mind and even jolt you awake." The latent mind is nonjudgmental; it offers you pure facts that you otherwise could not access. The overt, conscious mind, on the other hand, is extremely judgmental, clouds your vision, and prevents you from seeing facts and solutions clearly.

Try this process; you will begin to depend on it. Al promises, "The human mind will never let you down." His process will help clarify the vision for you, your prospects, and customers. Your intuition will come to guide your relationships, and support your vision, over time.

6. **Build Your Vision for the Long Term.** You must create a vision that you are willing to stand behind, and work for, over an extended period of time. There really is no such thing as an overnight success. Michael Jordan did not learn how to play basketball the day he joined the Chicago Bulls. Tiger Woods took thousands of practice swings before he won a major tournament. Everyone who wants to achieve mastery in a chosen profession must commit to a long-term vision and must support that vision over time. Being a true sales leader is not a one-time transaction; rather, it is a process of living and acting in a continuous state of belief, a state that supports the goals you are attempting to achieve now and over time. Each year we get older and our circumstances change; our needs may change as well. But our passion for the big things we want to accomplish on this earth should never die.

7. **Make Sure Your Vision Features the Element of Time.**
The element of time drives achievement. If there are no temporal limits on your goals, you tend to lose focus and you aren't accountable for your results. You—and everyone in your circle—should know when you plan to make the vision a reality. So, pick a date. That takes guts, of course, but such bravery is one of the prerequisites of leadership. John F. Kennedy, for example, challenged the nation to land a man on the moon before the 1960s were over. Not when we felt like getting around to it, mind you, but before that decade was out. That specificity made the vision all the more vivid.

Alternatively, if you're one of the people who prefers to state your goals as a present-tense assertion of what you bring to the world *right now*, you can do that. For example: "To stand out as a sales representative who exceeds customer expectations and quota consistently—week after week and quota after quota."

Personal Vision Versus Customer Vision

You must have a clear personal vision, *and* you must work with your client to develop a unique vision that's based on where that client wants to go. Before you start puking all over the place about your personal vision, find out how the customer sees the world and the results the customer is trying to attain! You must do this if you expect to:

- Attract your customer's time and attention.
- Win the alliances that will help you to deliver on the vision.
- Reduce your sales cycle.

You'll learn more about how to uncover the results your prospects and customers are after in Chapter 7.

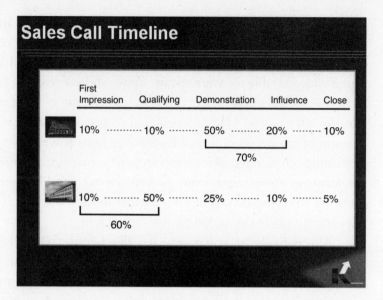

Figure 4.1

In the figure above, I make a case for the differences in the sales call timeline between the "old school" of selling and the leadership selling model that I advocate in this book. In later chapters of this book, I'll be using this model to illustrate all of the elements of the sales cycle.

Notice that the basic elements between the old way of selling and the new way are the same: first impression, qualifying, demonstration, influence, and close. The difference has to do with the element of vision and with the amount of time you spend in the various steps.

When I started selling copiers in 1980, we spent most of our training learning how to deliver demos, explain our features, and, of course, how to utter the (supposedly) magic words that would allow us to close the deal. The emphasis then was on presentation and closing.

Today, you need to spend more time in the first impression and qualifying stages building a shared vision with your prospect. This entails finding out how your customer views things, and what their vision is for the results they want to achieve. Once you've ascertained what these are, you will spend less time puking up facts about bells and whistles that may have no connection to your customer's world, and you will spend more time in discussion about the ways you can help them get to where they want to go, quickly and safely. You will therefore:

1. **Improve Your Positioning.** By starting the conversation around your customer's vision, you are automatically improving your position and differentiating yourself from the competition. While everyone else pukes up their features, you will be showing an interest and sincerity in helping your customers. Your prospects and customers will start feeling that "spontaneous combustion of caring" that I discussed in the previous chapter. By the time you are ready to explain how you might be able to work together, the prospect will be ready to listen with undivided attention, and your proposed solutions will land with greater impact.

2. **Uncover Hidden Traps.** This is the part they never taught us about when they trained us to sell copiers! All too often, salespeople start selling too fast or, as I've explained, puking up all the familiar reasons the customer should buy and then attempting to move to the close. Always be closing, right? Wrong! Here's the problem: If you try to close too soon, you may never get the opportunity to find out about the hidden objections that are standing in the way of your sale! Getting customers to speak about goals (short term

and long term) helps you learn what they want and don't want. You can't build a mutually inspiring vision without this information.

Remember, it is as important to hear about their fears as it is to hear about their desires. If we miss finding out any of this information before we start selling, there is an increased chance we will have missed a hidden objection or two. Often, we don't get a second chance. So find out as much as you can up front about the vision that is *currently* driving your customer's decision-making process. This one step can make the difference between closing the deal and not getting the business.

3. **Improve Your Closing Ratio.** When I started selling, a great deal of emphasis was placed on closing, and hardly any was placed on vision. There were books telling us the 101 best closes you were supposed to use. Most of them were very poorly disguised attempts to manipulate the prospect's insecurities. What a joke! Today, this type of selling simply won't fly. (I'm not sure it was all that effective back when I was selling copiers either.)

Leaders understand that closing is not a singular event that is based around one statement or question. Closing is a process; if you want to improve the numbers connected to that process, you must start with the vision.

The Leader's Advantage

Most of the people who think they have closing problems really have opening problems. They don't know how to open up the conversation and build a shared vision with the prospect. Only when they do that will their numbers improve.

Your Turn!

Now it's time for you to roll your sleeves up and get to work. Remember, the title of this book is *Lead, Sell, or Get Out of the Way*, it's time to start leading. You are not a spectator sitting in the stands. If you truly want to emerge as a sales leader, and sell more, you must get out on the field and play. Otherwise, you should count on getting out the way and letting your competition take over.

Personal Accountability

I cited personal accountability as the seventh trait of a successful sales leader. You and I will work our way up to that trait (it's got a chapter of its own at the end of this book), but along the way you will start demonstrating accountability in little steps. You will begin to document the ways that you are going to do things differently in order to attain different results, and that will start here.

On that note, let me ask you something important. What's going to happen when you finish this book? Is it going to find a spot on your bookcase? What are the chances you are going to keep looking at it once you've finished reading it for the first time? Maybe, you'll take a glance at it a few times. But we all know that, with our busy lives, once the book goes back on the bookshelf, it usually stays there. The ideas that once captivated us are forgotten forever.

This book is going to be different. At the end of every chapter, starting with this one, you will see a page called a Commitment Sheet. Feel free to make copies of this page; you may need several for each chapter. From this point forward, you are going to fill out a Commitment Sheet every time you complete a chapter. This sheet is for the commitments you will make to yourself about what you are going to do differently to get better sales results. Reading this book alone will not get you those results. Implementation of the best ideas will generate the results you are after.

> Commitment (Pronunciation: ko-'mit-mint, Function: noun, Definition: a: an agreement or pledge to do something in the future; b: something pledged; c: the state or an instance of being obligated or emotionally impelled, a commitment to a cause.)

    This chapter is all about a personal commitment to your *cause* and your vision. You will use your Commitment Sheet to launch your cause and to become crystal clear about the vision that is going to drive you to a new level of achievement. Then you are going to make each Commitment Sheet something you connect with at least once a week.

    You'll do this with each of the Commitment Sheets that appear at the end of each chapter. I don't much care how you use them; tear them out of the book, fold them up, put them in your pocket, write them in your Day-timer, or transcribe them and send them to yourself so you can read them on your Blackberry or iPhone. However you choose to connect with the work you've done, keep this material close to you for reference and measurement of your progress. If you want an electronic form of this sheet, please go to www.leadsellorgetoutoftheway.com and click on the Commitment Sheet button.

Your Chapter Four Commitment

Create a personal vision for yourself. It's okay to start with a five- or six-sentence vision. Once you have the main idea down, wordsmith it until it is concise, powerful, and capable of impelling you to action

Your personal vision statement should directly or indirectly answer this question: *What would success look like, feel like, and sound like for you?*

Remember, your vision can be stated in the present tense, as if you were living it right now. It can also be stated as something specific you are trying to accomplish by a certain point in time.

Here are some examples of good vision statements:

- To exceed customer expectations and a 60 percent market share by year's end.
- To have 5,010 members in good standing by January 1, 2010.
- To consistently deliver a 150 percent return on investment for my clients.

Remember, the above statements were not designed to compel you as an individual to action. They are merely samples. The trick is to create a statement that stirs *your* emotions, and inspires *you* to action whenever you come in contact with it.

It's time to create your vision statement. Brainstorm it on a separate sheet of paper if necessary, and insert it in the form on the next page, following the word "vision."

 **COMMITMENT!**

(Pronunciation: ko-'mit-mint, Function: noun, Definition: a: an agreement or pledge to do something in the future; b: something pledged c: the state or an instance of being obligated or emotionally impelled, a commitment to a cause)

VISION:_____

_____

_____

_____

_____

_____

_____

_____

_____

_____

_____

_____

_____

_____

_____

_____

_____

_____

_____

_____

For more of these sample sheets go to http://www.leadsellorgetoutoftheway.com.

Figure 4.2   Commitment Sheet

5 | Positioning

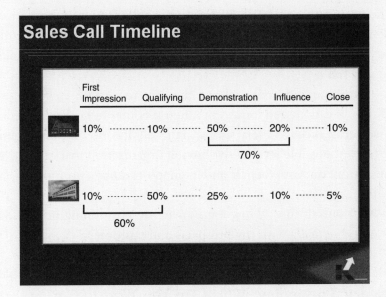

Figure 5.1

As we have learned, sales leaders are purpose driven, not task driven. Their primary focus is on *outcomes*. That means their first step is positioning, establishing themselves as high on the priority list, and critical to the success of the organization. This is the first step in the leader's sales cycle. Positioning allows leaders to set the stage for working on purpose and eliminates unnecessary time investments that do not support them strategically.

Look at Figure 5.1 on the previous page. The sales leader's timeline appears on the bottom, while the "standard selling cycle" is shown at the top. Notice that the very first step is called First Impression. Determining the First Impression you want to leave—and then leaving it—is what positioning is all about.

Believe it: The way you start the process really does help determine how well you finish it! Positioning determines who you will talk to, what you will talk about, what products/services you are most likely to sell, how much of it you are going to sell, and how quickly you will sell it.

There's an old saying about the key to success in real estate: location, location, and location. When it comes to leadership selling, the secret to success is very similar. For you, location means targeting the highest possible level of the buying organization that can and will take action on your behalf and then positioning, positioning, and positioning.

Ask yourself this: "How am I currently positioning myself *strategically* and *tactically* with my prospects and customers?"

Strategic Positioning: Where Do You Want to Go?

The word strategically refers to the playing field on which you choose to compete. Too often sales executives play small. They play the same game their competitors are playing. They call at or near the lowest possible buying level of the organization, and they look for rules to follow. Leaders, on the other hand, call high and with purpose . . . and set their own rules.

> ### The Leader's Advantage
>
> Leaders position themselves strategically as a resource for achieving better—not the same—results than those the prospect or customer is currently experiencing. Usually, that means changing the rules of game or even creating a whole new game!

If you concentrate on playing at a higher level than your competition and providing results your competition is not even thinking about, the end result for you will be little or no competition. If you continue to play the same game that your competitors are playing, however, you'll find yourself with more competition than you know what to do with.

Changing the game is a big part of strategic positioning. Although certain procurement processes may have been identified, leaders never assume that those are the processes they have to follow. Do you remember the chemical company I talked about a little earlier in the book? At the start of the selling process, the customer was all set with a bidding process that was supposedly mandatory. That changed!

The process changed because we had strategically repositioned my client as an invaluable *partner* to this customer. As a result, two interesting things happened: First, many of the bid elements were based on my client's specifications. Second, when the other competitors couldn't meet one of the requirements of the bid, the customer revoked the supposedly hard-and-fast rules and, negotiated a deal directly with my client! Chalk it all up to effective early positioning in that sales cycle.

Let's look more closely at the strategy half of the positioning equation; the part where you choose the type of field you will play on.

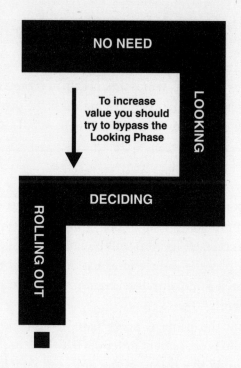

To increase
value you should
try to bypass the
Looking Phase

NO NEED

LOOKING

DECIDING

ROLLING OUT

Figure 5.2   Four Buying Phases™

We can break a customer's buying cycle into four phases (see Figure 5.2):

- No Need
- Looking
- Deciding
- Rolling Out

Most salespeople make a huge strategic positioning error by searching out customers who are in the active phase of looking for a new product/service. In this phase, the prospect has already identified a need and is looking for a solution. If you plan to enter into the buying cycle at this phase, you'd better be ready for a struggle;

unless you helped create the specifications for the potential solution, you are going to be trapped in a commodity sale that will lead to a knock-down, drag-out battle that pits your features and price against your competitors'. This is a contest in which there may be lots of contenders, but only one winner. Be realistic. What are your chances of winning that fight? How many of these battles have you participated in already? What percentage have you actually won?

The fact is targeting customers who are actively engaged in looking for solutions is not a sales strategy that is based on your value. To the contrary, it is a completely transactional strategy. This does not mean you shouldn't go for the deal if you happen to stumble into one of these situations. Of course, there are some sales arenas—home repair services, for instance—that typically won't have a deal unless something breaks. Even in that situation, though, how you position yourself matters. What we're talking about here is how to make the most of the job of positioning when your best active selling opportunity arises or even long before that point.

Let's say you're a homeowner. If your air conditioner breaks down, who will you call? What vendor is at the top of your list? Is there one? Leaders are inclined to win that top spot, not by addressing a single narrow problem with the prospect, but by defining the prospect's larger purpose and matching it up to their own. They want to lead the customer through the process of acquisition, not act as a mere participant in a role, like supplier of products and services. They want to be the trusted advisor to whom customers look to help them define solutions that will create better results.

If your purpose is to sell valued outcomes to your customers, to help them get to the next level of success, to become an invaluable resource, and to capture the lion's share of your customer's supply needs, then your positioning strategy cannot be transactional!

You should be looking for solutions to enhance the prospect's overall enterprise—the entire situation that your prospect faces—without being limited to any one need or product/service offering. If you really are a leader, you must be willing and eager to look at the bigger picture.

No Need

When was the last time you called on a prospect who said he had "no need"? Did you assume there really was no opportunity there, and simply move on? That's a huge mistake, one that you won't see a sales leader making.

The Leader's Advantage

The words "no need" do not equate to "no opportunity"! You must do what the sales leader does and listen to the *intent* of the words you hear.

Consider this scenario: You start talking about computers. The prospect has no current computer issues that need resolving, so the prospect says some variation on the magic words "We have no need/no interest/no application for what you're offering."

Before you move on, though, you consider the underlying *intent* of his words and realize he is actually saying this: "I really don't want to talk about computers with you." That's fine, but the simple fact that the prospect's computers are working right now doesn't mean that those computers are providing *all* of the possible outcomes the prospect may have on his wish list.

For instance, a prospect who puts up with a tolerably fast Internet connection may actually want a faster connection. Let's assume that's the case here. You probably would not learn about the Internet speed issue by simply talking about the hardware. In order to find out about any unrelated issues, you would have to respond to the "no need" response with a more creative question, one that might sound like this: "I understand that you have no current needs; but if you could improve three things in your current computer operation, what would those three things be?"

Congratulations! You've just positioned yourself strategically.

Granted, creating and delivering this kind of position for yourself takes a little practice, but once you learn how, you will see that it is comparatively easy to turn a "no need" response into a conversation.

Now, let's suppose you get a summary of the three things the prospect would wish for, one of which is a faster Internet connection. You have increased this sales opportunity by asking better questions. Before too long you're having a better exchange with the prospect, and eventually he starts thinking about why it might make sense to take action on that Internet speed thing sooner rather than later.

Think once again about those four buying phases. At this point, the prospect can go one of two ways. He can go into a looking mode, comparing all competitive offerings that have to do with increasing his Internet speed. If he goes that route, at least he's now doing the comparison with your spec in mind. You will have a higher level of influence than the other competitors who come along after you leave and are simply bidding on features and price! (That's the position you made a strategic decision to avoid by asking that creative question when you heard "no need," remember?)

Alternatively, the prospect can bypass the looking phase and go straight to the deciding phase, where he will start negotiating a contract with you so he can proceed to rollout with you as soon as possible!

Believe me, this does happen. As a general rule, though, it only happens to sales leaders. When it happens to you, you will know that you've made a sale based on *value*, not on price or features. You also will have created a relationship which will allow you to sell more to this customer in a shorter amount of time than you would have if you simply entered in the looking mode. During the looking phase, you usually are dealing with a transactional sale based around one product or service. By positioning yourself properly during the "no need" phase, you generally will uncover opportunities that will affect the whole enterprise and give yourself at least the chance to win a bigger chunk of this buyer's total expenditures.

While you may not be able to avoid the looking phase entirely, you certainly don't want to go out searching for street fights every working day. Amazingly, though, that's what the vast majority of professional salespeople end up doing because they wait until they run into someone who is looking for a solution and (of course) end up fighting with competitors.

What I'm suggesting may feel unfamiliar—at first. Remember, no new skill *starts out* feeling familiar and secure. Once upon a time, riding a bicycle was unfamiliar to you. You may even have considered it scary. But you took action, you learned the new skill, and you broadened what you could do by pushing up against your comfort zone just a little bit. That's exactly what you need to do here. (By the way, you'll learn more about how leaders ask effective questions in Chapter Seven.)

You May Still Get Stuck in the "Looking Phase"

Remember, when a buyer goes into a looking phase, she has already been influenced by someone or something. She has made up her mind as to what she's actually looking for. Ideally, that's *not* the point at which you, as a salesperson, want to meet her for the first time. The reality is, however, you sometimes can't help it.

Let's say, for example, that a potential customer's air conditioning breaks down, and the homeowner calls in three vendors for quotes. Many salespeople actively look for this point of entry in the purchasing cycle, because they feel this is the point at which the customer has a definite need and is looking to buy. Actually, this point of entry is littered with the carcasses of dead air-conditioner salespeople! These are the salespeople who have tripped over each other trying to impress the customer with their features—and discounted all of the profit out of the deal in the vain hope of getting a sale.

If you are in a situation where you must sell to someone who is looking—evaluating vendors—your goal should always be to position yourself as a resource who can create a more powerful, far-reaching solution, a solution that will separate you from the competition. So in the case of the air conditioning example, you wouldn't just ask the standard questions everyone else is asking, like "How many bedrooms do you need to cover?" Instead, you'd ask something like this: "Can you describe the three most important things that you need your new air conditioner to do?" Or, get even more specific: "Obviously, you want cold air, otherwise I wouldn't be here talking to you. What about other things, like energy savings or noise abatement? How important are those issues to you?"

That's not what most salespeople do when they run into someone who's in the looking phase, though. What most salespeople do is think, "Thank Heavens! I've finally got a live one!" Then they position themselves as commodity players. They do this by asking a couple of stupid questions that they've asked literally hundreds of times before, and then not listening very closely—or at all—to the answers. When the customer stops replying, the salesperson starts puking up the features and benefits that are virtually identical to what the competition is offering. Before you know it, the customer is trying to differentiate the vendors, and of course she does that the only way she knows how: by asking for better terms.

This is the cost of terrible positioning. Even if you get this order—and you're the last air conditioner salesperson still standing—are you sure this was the deal you wanted?

Tactical Positioning: What Do You Say and Do in Support of Your Strategy?

Now that you've learned the importance of strategic positioning we can discuss the *tactics* you will use. These are, in essence, the words you speak and the actions you take to get where you want to go.

There are three basic strategies to choose from when it comes to tactical positioning: title, product/service, and resource. Which one are you using right now?

Positioning by Title

Positioning exclusively by title is a common mistake among sales-people. As a group, salespeople can be highly creative when it comes to the job titles they mention to prospects and customers. You have probably heard (and perhaps created or been asked to adopt) your own fair share of these: account manager, senior strategic account specialist, regional manager (for a salesperson covering a region), and so on.

Positioning by (inflated) title alone almost always leads to a commodity sales situation. The prospect usually resents the attempt to gain status (and mislead) by means of an impressive-sounding title. Because your contact is usually eager to get back to the pressing business of the day, he or she will resolve that resentment by thinking, "Yeah, right, senior consultant, whatever," and by asking some variation on the following: "All right, let's cut to the chase; how much does it cost?" Welcome to commodity-level selling!

You cannot differentiate yourself by title alone. There are so many competitors out there that it's silly to try. After all, what truly separates one financial advisor from the other? You would never know simply from the title. I know plenty of home-based entrepreneurs who expect the simple recitation of the title "CEO" to open doors automatically. It won't—unless your name is Donald Trump! But even then, the name, title, and prestige will only guarantee Mr. Trump a meeting. It will not guarantee him the business!

A famous company name may well buy you an interview with the prospect. But will that guarantee you business? Don't count on it. Name brands do make it easier for you to get in the door. But at the end of the day, it is the perceived outcome that will carry the day. Even highly recognized brands can (and do) lose market share in a hurry.

What's wrong with relying on brand recognition to get the meeting? Nothing! But once that meeting starts, you must be ready to face the question: How will you continue the job of positioning yourself? How will you continue to win the other person's undivided attention? You only achieve that when the prospect believes the conversation is truly going to impact his or her life positively. How are you going to make that case? Your title and your company name won't make it for you!

Positioning by Product or Service

If you can't differentiate yourself from the competition by title, then the best way to achieve position yourself must be through your products and services, right? Wrong!

If I were the head of a medium-sized manufacturing firm, and you called me and told me that you specialized in "sales training" and wanted to talk to me for half an hour or so, what do you think my reaction would be? Well, I would probably start to shut down on you the moment I heard the phrase "sales training." Your call would have been the sixth one I'd received about sales training that week. I'd remind myself that thousands of other people also offer sales training ... I can call any of them any time I want, so why should I spend any of my valuable time listening to you?

The only thing we achieve by positioning ourselves by means of our products and services is to draw attention to the fact that we occupy a playing field that is crowded with competitors. That's true whether you sell computers, real estate, web site development, insurance, the ability to fix cavities, or high-performance windshield wipers. Simply identifying the products and services in which we specialize delivers no differentiation over our competitors. There are thousands of dentists who fill cavities, hundreds of web site developers who create web pages, and countless real estate agents who sell homes. The same holds true for most every product or service category. You have to do more than tell the person what you do or what you make.

Want to move out of commodity-selling mode and into solution selling? Then you need to position yourself as an invaluable resource. Don't talk to me about sales training—talk to me about an idea you have for improving my sales team's closing ratio!

Positioning by Resource

As a resource, you don't put the emphasis on what you call yourself or on the specific elements of the product or service you are offering. Instead, you highlight the *results* your customers will realize from using your unique mix of products and services. That's the reason you want to have a conversation in the first place; you want to talk about the results you've delivered!

This is immensely important, especially when you are dealing with prospects who have not worked with you before. At the very beginning of a relationship, prospects are more interested in what your products and services will actually provide than they are in virtually anything else. You must demonstrate that the product or service you offer—and you yourself—should be considered a resource that will aid in the attainment of key goals.

What do I mean by resource? Let me explain. As a resource, you must address at least one of the following four areas (see Figure 5.3):

1. *Improved Revenues*: Can the products and services you offer help your customers generate more revenues? This value affects all types of sales. A financial advisor provides improved revenues through higher returns on investment. A search

engine specialist provides improved revenues through an increase of visitors to a given site. There are countless other products and services that generate more business; you must prove that yours does as well.

2. *Improved Productivity*: Some organizations and individuals specialize in providing productivity gains. My colleague, the author Laura Stack, who is known as the Productivity Pro®, helps her clients achieve maximum results in minimum time and improve their personal productivity. How valuable is that for an organization or an individual? Whether productivity takes the form of reducing the amount of time spent re-entering invoice information, or of providing a home that allows people to live fuller, more satisfying lives, this is a powerful appeal that can generate instant attention and interest.

3. *Reduced Operating Costs*: Sometimes, what matters most to a prospect or customer is not how much you make, but how much you have left over at the end of the day. Reducing costs can move a company from the red to the black, improve a state's bond rating, and make the difference between poverty and prosperity for a young family. Ask yourself this: Can the products and services you offer reduce the overall operating costs of your customers? How?

I'm not talking about offering the lowest price. I'm talking about helping your customer reduce his or her overall cost of operation by providing better quality products and services. For example, a dentist can reduce his patients' costs by creating a crown. If the dentist is known for quality work and for producing crowns that fit properly and last longer than those of other dentists, then the patient is likely to spend less money down the road in replacement costs—even if the price is initially higher than the competition's. I know this first hand since I recently had all my crowns redone! I chose the dentist

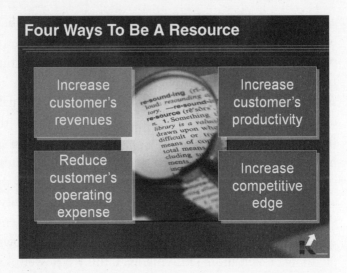

Figure 5.3

who had the best reputation—and the highest price—because
I knew I did not want to have the job done again.

4. *Increased Competitive Edge*: Can the products and services you
offer help your customers gain a competitive edge or improve
the edge they currently have? Senior executives are usually
obsessed with the question of how they can outperform and
outsmart the competition. If you can assist your customers in
this area, then you have the basis for an appeal that will instantly differentiate you from your own competition. A dentist
creating a radiant smile through cosmetic dentistry is definitely
giving you a competitive advantage, especially if you're a network news anchor or someone else whose physical appearance
is important to professional success. The health and beauty aid
industry is another classic example of this. They're not selling
the ingredients; they are selling the sizzle, the outcome, the
shiny hair, the full lips, the bright eyes, and that competitive
appearance advantage we all want.

Your "Resource Proclamation"

As a sales leader, you're going to be using a tool that I call a Resource Proclamation to position yourself as a resource and get the relationship off on the right foot.

The Leader's Advantage

A Resource Proclamation is a carefully designed initial positioning statement.

Your Resource Proclamation will allow you to begin the conversation from a broad, 30,000-foot perspective. Isn't that how most leaders you've run into tend to talk at the beginning of a relationship? It may not be possible for you to talk about all four areas where you can identify yourself as a resource within this statement, and it may not be wise to try. For one thing, you may not know much yet about the prospect. Keep it simple!

The Leader's Wisdom

"In our end is our beginning."—T.S. Eliot

The way you begin the discussion really will affect the direction and conclusion of that discussion. Start big, start broad, and start by addressing *only* elements that help to establish you as a resource. Remember, whenever you find yourself talking about something that does not directly connect to advantages like improving productivity, reducing operating costs, improving revenues, or winning a competitive edge, you have just lost the other person's attention!

At the outset of the relationship, you must offer your customers and prospects a realistic possibility of improving their results in *at least one* of the four resource areas discussed above. Your Resource Proclamation allows you to do this and is an essential prerequisite to positioning. Each sales leader must develop his or her own unique proclamation; you can't use someone else's.

Creating a Resource Proclamation is a significant personal investment of time and energy. The payoff will not look like much on paper: one or two powerful sentences. Creating those brief sentences will take some time and effort, but it will be time well spent. There are a lot of variables to consider, and there are usually a lot of blind alleys to avoid. In many cases, your products and solutions will address more than one resource area. For example, if your services increase your customer's productivity, there is a good chance that you can also reduce her operating costs and improve her revenues. Which should you mention in the first one or two minutes of the conversation? You don't know yet. It will take time and some experimentation to develop the right Resource Proclamation. But you *must* take this step! This Resource Proclamation is one of the key tactics that Timber Trading sales executive Rodger Ekstrom used to reposition his company—and himself. Telling a customer who owns a lumber yard that you are there to help him increase market share is a much, much more powerful way of launching the relationship than talking about a particular product, such as Eastern White Pine, and it's certainly more powerful than talking about your own title.

To create a Resource Proclamation that establishes you as an invaluable resource, you must think beyond the features, functions and benefits that your products and services offer the user. Think about what happens as a result of your solutions. Think about the cumulative effect on the organization or an individual within it. The results you offer are what people who have the power and are in a position to buy want to hear about. How you deliver the results is also important, but bear in mind that that's the second thing prospects want to know. If you don't get through the first step of gaining interest, time, and attention, you won't be invited to explain how you do it!

How I Created My First Resource Proclamation

For years I told potential clients that I was a professional speaker (that's a title) who specialized in sales, negotiations, and customer service training (all products). The prospects usually responded by asking me a very simple question: How was I different from the thousands of speakers offering the same things? During my first three years in business, I struggled to find the answer to that question. Then, one day, while I was on-site with a client, it hit me.

A successful marketing research firm had hired me to give a two-day sales seminar for all of their top management and account managers. After spending the first morning on sales training issues, the president of the firm interrupted me to ask a question: "Ron, let's cut to the chase. How do I sell my market research services to the CEO of a Fortune 100 company who really believes in my quality, but cannot take the risk of losing confidential information? We often conduct projects for clients who are competitors to each other. My client's biggest fear is that if he provides any outsider with information that may inadvertently be leaked to the competition, he could seriously damage his company's competitive position. So here's what I want to know, Ron. How do we get past that objection?"

I offered to role-play the scenario with him. He launched some tough objections, and I addressed each of them by posing tailored questions that fit the CEO's situation perfectly. At the end of our role-playing session, my contact threw his hands up in the air and said, "You've got all the answers, Ron. I need to bottle you up and take you on every sales call." I pointed out that I really hadn't offered any answers during the role-play, but I had asked a better sequence of questions than his account managers had been asking.

As the words left my mouth, I knew what made me different from every other sales trainer, consultant, and speaker I'd ever run into: my focus on effective questioning.

There was still a problem, however. I had to take my customers' perceptions into account. If senior executives felt their challenges had nothing to do with questions—and I knew that most of them did—how could I reach them? It's a core philosophy of mine that asking enough of the right questions is crucial to success in sales, leadership, negotiations, and customer service. Yet, if the *customer* did not perceive questions to be an important issue, my initial emphasis on the question-based approach was going to be irrelevant! Was this really how I wanted to begin the conversation? I didn't think so.

Eager to improve my opening, I fine-tuned it over the next weeks and months and took a little of my own medicine by asking myself a critical question: As a result of learning how to ask more effective questions, what did my clients achieve? The answers were always related to growth—in some cases, fairly dramatic growth—in revenues and profits. Once I took the time to look at these results, I realized that what my clients were buying from me was not so much a product or service, and not even my own expertise on the art of questioning, but rather the results of getting new customers, increasing sales to existing customers, negotiating win-win agreements, and providing new levels of service. Of course, the challenge was communicating all of this information to my prospects and customers at the opening of a sales call in a way that would gain their time and attention in a matter of just a few seconds.

In working on my own Resource Proclamation, I went through an exercise with a colleague during which I had to write out dozens of statements describing the results attained by my clients that were a direct result of the techniques I taught them. It took a while to come up with them, but the results were worth it! By looking at those statements, I was able to distinguish a common pattern. In every success I had ever delivered, my clients were able to increase their revenues, market share, and profitability as a result of having worked with me on questioning and related techniques. These three common elements were combined into the following Resource Proclamation—a single, powerful sentence that literally took me months to develop: *I help organizations dominate their markets and help people get closer to the people they serve.*

What company doesn't want to dominate its markets and get closer to its customers? This Resource Proclamation, which evolved from the initial discovery of my own skills in training others in questioning techniques, supports two of the critical resource areas I shared with you earlier in this chapter: increasing profits (through revenues and market share) and attaining the competitive edge. This is what I do—expressed in the language of leadership!

I remember calling up a manager at a major hotel chain, a man who had hired me in the past to speak to his group. I asked him what he thought of my new Resource Proclamation. His response was immediate and dramatic: "Ron, market domination is exactly what I want to buy. I don't care how you do it when you are in here giving the presentation, as long as it is ethical and customer focused. But I definitely want to increase my market share."

That was more than a decade ago. In the years since I developed my first draft, I've learned a lot, and I've fine-tuned my Resource Proclamation several times. Each time I've fine-tuned it, I've brought it closer to the concerns of my ideal prospect.

The Leader's Wisdom

In the factory we make cosmetics; in the drugstore we sell hope.—Charles Revson

I remember a time when I was sitting next to a gentleman on an airplane, and he asked me what I did for a living. I gave him an early version of my Resource Proclamation, one that focused on how I helped companies to dominate their markets. He said, "Hmm ... that sounds rather illegal." I said, "What are you talking about?" He told me that in Europe companies shy away from using words like "dominate" because of their sensitivity to giving the perception of collusion. This gave me an entirely new perspective on the way that I had worded my proclamation. Sometimes it definitely helps to get another person's opinion!

Fine-Tune It!

I learned from this gentleman's comments—and from years of working with this particular motto—that you cannot simply develop a statement like this and consider it done. Once you come up with your Resource Proclamation, you must be ready to fine-tune it. Just as in marketing, this is all about testing. No matter how great you think your statement sounds, what *really* matters is whether the customer truly understands your intent. Of course, you will also want to update your Resource Proclamation from time to time to make sure it reflects the way you do business now, and the impact of any new products or services you may have added to your offerings since you last revised it. In my situation, my business has now evolved far beyond sales training. As an advisor to boards and senior executives, my services often involve higher-level projects. Sales training is still something we do, but it is only one of several ways we help our clients achieve their outcomes.

Here's what my Resource Proclamation looks like right now: *I help organizations and individuals sell more in less time at higher profit.*

And here's another variation: *I help build and maintain high-performing sales cultures.*

The better you understand the value that you bring to the market, the more likely you are to see opportunities to tweak and refine your Resource Proclamation. You must constantly ask yourself, "What will resonate at the highest possible level and at the same time touch on one or more of the four resource areas?" Your answer to that question should always be evolving. You will never be finished with the job of developing and honing your resource proclamation. That is how I came up with my current declaration—by being ready to fine-tune the old one. And you can bet that I am working right now on my next version!

Beware of Preconceptions!

The biggest obstacle that we typically face in creating an initial Resource Proclamation is our own deeply entrenched preconceptions about what will or won't establish us as a resource for our clients.

We often fixate on minor details or specialized areas of interest that are powerful for us and assume that by talking about these things we are establishing ourselves as a resource in one of the areas I shared with you earlier. However, there are usually some dots that still need to be connected.

For example, one of my clients considers himself an expert on American presidents. When he started marketing himself as "the presidential expert," he did not attract as big a market as he had hoped for. I asked him, "Who really cares if you're an expert on the presidents? What improvements will people realize in their lives by learning from your expertise?" He thought about that for a while and then started positioning himself as a resource who develops leaders with presidential skills. What is the resource area he is addressing with such an appeal? Competitive advantage! He helps people achieve their professional goals by coaching them to compete—and lead—successfully.

He made the transition from what he was interested in to a resource area his prospects were interested in.

Resource Proclamations come in a couple of different flavors. Let's look at these variations now.

The Global Resource Proclamation

A *Global Resource Proclamation* is intended to win time, interest, and attention from the very first seconds of a conversation with a potential client, even in a case when you may know little or nothing about the person you're talking to. This is a non-targeted version of the Resource Proclamation that is designed to work well in almost any situation you find yourself. Because you do not know anything about the issues facing the person you are speaking with, your Global Resource Proclamation must address one or more resource areas in a generic manner.

Suppose, for example, that you are at a cocktail party and someone asks you what you do. You could respond saying you are a financial planner, or you could use a Global Resource Proclamation and say, "I help people fund their dreams."

The resource area that this statement covers is profits—making more money to fund other initiatives. What's the other person going to say? Probably something like "That's interesting; how do you do that?"

Here are sample Global Resource Proclamations for several industries.

If you're at a gathering where someone asks you what you do for a living, don't reply with a boring "I'm a sales rep." Do what a leader does: offer your Global Resource Proclamation! It may sound strange. It may even sound corny. Anytime you try something new, it will sound a little odd to your ear the first time. Experiment and

> ### Sample Global Resource Proclamations
>
> Financial Services:
>
> "I help clients fund their dreams."
>
> Computers:
>
> "I provide customers with a technically competitive advantage."
>
> Architects:
>
> "I transform clients' visions into affordable reality."

take your Global Resource Proclamation out for a test drive. See what happens! If it sounds a little out of the ordinary, that might be a good thing. Remember that one of the skills leaders excel at is getting—and keeping—people's attention.

Ingredients of a Successful Global Resource Proclamation

Your global Resource Proclamation should accomplish three things.

1. *Communicate the "what" without generating a "So what?" response.* The Global Resource Proclamation should convey the bottom-line benefits and value that your customer will gain from a relationship with you. It should not describe how you offer what you offer. If your Global Resource Proclamation is on target, it should prompt your customer to *ask you for more information.*

   To make sure your global Resource Proclamation passes the "so what" test, ask yourself this: "If I heard this for the first time, would I ask 'So what?' in response?"

For instance: If you were to say to me, "I provide people with cutting-edge computer technology," my response to you would be "So what? What does cutting-edge computer technology do for me?" A better way to communicate the same message might sound like this: *"I provide cutting-edge technology that quickly transforms businesses into lean, mean fighting machines."*

In the example above, you are now linking your efforts to two of the four resource areas, increased productivity and reduced operating costs, and you're implying progress on a third front: competitive advantage. Most people want to increase their efficiency, reduce their costs, and increase their competitive advantage. You are now communicating the message that you can help them do so, and you're doing that in a compelling way. The specific example I've just shared with you, of course, probably isn't right for you, but the process by which you'll develop your Resource Proclamation is definitely right.

2. *Keep it simple!* In this day of Blackberrys and instant virtual meetings, attention spans are short. That means your Global Resource Proclamation must be easily understood in a matter of just a few seconds if it is to create impact. You must hold your audience's attention. I have seen thousands of sales representatives kill opportunities by going into long statements about what they represent, and by "long" I mean more than 30 seconds! If your Resource Proclamation takes you between 30 and 120 seconds to deliver, it still needs work. It is literally a waste of your breath.

3. *Make it memorable.* Your Global Resource Proclamation must be something that sticks in people's heads. It has to be strong enough to create a lasting impression that someone will remember and be able to communicate easily to other people days, weeks, or months after you say it—*once*. Your goal should

be to increase the number of people who can remember exactly what you do for a living after having met you a single time. Your goal should be to leave the person motivated to remember exactly what you say and who you are and to talk about you to other people.

The Leader's Advantage

Your Resource Proclamation must be so powerful that it stops prospects in their tracks, wins you their full attention, and gets them to ask you to tell them more. If your Resource Proclamation doesn't do all that . . . it still needs work!

Communicating your value as a potential resource to anyone and everyone you meet in a matter of seconds takes practice, and it's definitely not easy at first. Talking about yourself this concisely and directly will not be your first instinct and may make you a bit uncomfortable. Remember, however, that leaders know how to embrace positive change. Learning to speak dramatically and effectively about what you do for a living needs to be part of your DNA. Practice this!

The Situational Resource Proclamation

A Global Resource Proclamation is a great start, but it's not enough. There will also be times when you will consistently call on the same prospects and customers. Obviously, you will not want to keep repeating a given phrase over and over again at the beginning of each meeting; yet you will still face the same challenge of gaining the time, interest, and attention of your contact. You will still have to communicate in just a few seconds how this meeting is going to be of value to her, and you must do so using a new message.

This brings us to the *Situational* Resource Proclamation. Let's suppose that you are meeting a current customer to introduce a new product. Instead of saying, "I have something new to show you," why not say something like this: *"We have just developed a cutting-edge product that your peers are using right now to reduce costs by between 10 and 30 percent."*

Now *that* will win your customer's time, interest, and attention! Obviously, you must develop Situational Resource Proclamations with care and attention, and with due consideration for what you know this person's hot buttons to be. You can create Situational Resource Proclamations for specific buying mindsets; here are some examples to consider.

Situational Resource Proclamation for Someone Who Is Strongly Focused on Comparing Vendors

"I want to share a new technology that is best in class and generates a great ROI." People in this mindset are all about the comparison. They want to know how your product and service stands up against competitive offerings.

Situational Resource Proclamation for Someone Who Is Strongly Focused on Making the Right Decision

"I want to share a new technology that has dramatically cut costs for some of your peers in the industry." These people are all about the results. They want to know how they are going to be better off by choosing to work with you.

Situational Resource Proclamation for a Potential End User

"I want to share with you a new technology that is going to be easier to use and create fewer problems." This is what this person wants to hear: How is your new product/service going to make the job easier?

I'll be sharing more with you on all three of these mindsets in Chapter Six. Right now, you must be ready to develop multiple Situational Resource Proclamations, each targeted to an individual contact, for each new product or service you come out with.

Resource Proclamation Dos and Don'ts

- **Do** *make sure the proclamation sounds authentic and spontaneous.* If it sounds canned, then there's a problem. If your statement does not get the customer to start opening up, then you need to tweak it. Sometimes that means changing one word; sometimes more in-depth changes are necessary. Regardless, the Resource Proclamation must become a part of who you are and what your business offers, and you must deliver this message in a genuine manner.
- **Do** *be ready to edit your proclamation down after your first draft.* When I work with audiences, I will sometimes get a Resource Proclamation that sounds like this:

    "Hi, my name is Missy Jones, and I work for XYZ Corp. We build high-quality products that pass all the tests and will add value to your organization. They will make your job easier and help you sell more in the marketplace. They will also help you compete."

    This is way too long. The key ideas are high quality, make job easier, sell more, and compete. All of the other words are dispensable. And putting your name and your company name in the Resource Proclamation does not help you; your client is already aware of this very basic information. Consider this revision: *I want to share some ideas on how to improve your quality, simplify your job, generate more revenues, and increase your competitive edge.*

or

I am here to help you sell more, improve your market position, and make your life easier.

Again, remember the power of the word "share." People like it when others share with them; they don't enjoy being dictated to.

■ ***Don't*** *use the Resource Proclamation as an excuse to launch into a sales monologue.* Remember, the sole purpose of the Resource Proclamation is to gain your customers' time and attention, not to sell to them on the spot. This is not the time to puke all over the prospect. You want to get the prospect or customer to respond in a way that opens up a dialogue and allows you to ask good questions. (I'll show you exactly what constitutes a good question in Chapter Seven.)

Why You Need the Resource Proclamation

The products you sell are of the utmost importance to you; however, your customers have other concerns that are important to them. The only way you will succeed in aligning your purpose with your customer's purpose—and winning people's time and attention—is to verbalize a powerful message that identifies you as a potential resource for addressing his or her current challenges. The Resource Proclamation, whether global or situational, is that message.

The following is a step-by-step guide to developing and perfecting your Resource Proclamation. Remember, it's never done!

Your Chapter Five Commitment

1. Commit some time to creating your Global and Situational Resource Proclamations, using the Commitment Sheet on the next page. Spend the time you need to get this right!

2. Come up with at least 20 positive outcomes that your products, services, and company offer your clients. Write them all down. This is not the time to analyze. Just keep writing! Make sure all of your ideas are expressed in complete sentences.

3. Identify the two or three most common themes you see.

4. Use these themes to create at least one Global Resource Proclamation for a person you are planning to meet for the very first time and three powerful Situational Resource Proclamations for people you have met at least once. Remember, each Resource Proclamation should encourage people to respond with "Tell me more!" instead of "So what?"

5. Over the course of a week, use the Global Resource Proclamation identified at least 10 times in live sales discussions with a new prospect or decision maker who has not yet met you. Try to use your three Situational Resource Proclamations at least five times during that same week with people you already know.

6. Pick the Resource Proclamations that feel most effective and natural to you. Keep tweaking them until they naturally roll off of your tongue and cause people to say, "That's interesting; tell me more!" Be ready to edit, revise, and tweak your Resource Proclamations as time goes on. Accept that this is an ongoing process, requiring at least a monthly review. Whenever you get a Resource Proclamation that does a better job of conveying exactly where you add value, start using it!

 **COMMITMENT!**

(Pronunciation: ko-'mit-mint, Function: noun, Definition: a: an agreement or pledge to do something in the future; b: something pledged c: the state or an instance of being obligated or emotionally impelled, a commitment to a cause)

_____

_____

_____

_____

_____

_____

_____

_____

_____

_____

_____

_____

_____

_____

_____

_____

_____

_____

_____

_____

_____

For more of these sample sheets go to http://www.leadsellorgetoutoftheway.com.

Figure 5.4   Commitment Sheet

6 | Building Alliances

Great salespeople get better and better over time, and one of the areas that they're constantly improving is their ability to build and support new alliances. Mediocre and poor salespeople are usually stagnant when it comes to creating and maintaining new professional connections. They wonder why they should even bother establishing new relationships when they can rely on a few "proven" contacts.

However, forming new connections is an essential leadership skill, particularly these days, when companies merge or are swallowed up at a brisk pace and people change jobs and careers quickly. A single, seemingly safe list of "old reliable" contacts can change from active to obsolete in a matter of days. Another technological and competitive reason to make new contacts has to do with today's advanced communication technologies. After all, your competition is seeking new connections by texting, e-mailing, and Googling your prospects and customers! The seller with the best "coverage" will usually be the one who's best positioned for success.

The fact is that you need multiple points of contact—and not only within the company you're trying to sell. No matter how many connections you now have in your world, it's not enough. You need to know how to build more, and you need to know how to support and expand your existing alliances. If you are not willing to improve your ability to create such relationships, then you should be ready to give up your seat at the table to someone who is.

As a leader, you will want to focus on three areas in particular: internal alliances, customer alliances, and advocate alliances. Let's look at each now.

Building Internal Alliances

Building internal alliances means creating associations at the place where you work on behalf of your customers and prospects—a process that salespeople sometimes make more difficult than it has to be.

The Leader's Wisdom

"Organizations have more to fear from lack of quality internal customer service than from any level of external customer service."—Ron Tillotson

One of the reasons that we occasionally run into trouble getting help from our own team may be our own attitudes. Let's face it: Salespeople have, at times, earned a reputation within their own organizations of being arrogant, self-centered, manipulative, and overaggressive when it comes to dealing with the people they work with. If any static like that surrounds your own interactions with your colleagues, it's time to stop debating about whether or not the perceptions your coworkers have are true, fair, or accurate and start building bridges that will allow you to act together harmoniously. You don't just need external allies; you need internal allies, as well.

Here's a true story that will show you *why* you need good internal and external allies. When I was selling electronic time stamps for a major manufacturer in that industry back in the dim, dark period before the dawn of the Information Age, one of our markets was the financial services industry. The organizations in this field used our time-stamps on every trader's desk to ensure that the time of a given order matched the transaction time exactly. With millions of dollars on the line and tight regulations governing when and how trades could be conducted, these companies had to protect themselves.

I was a new sales representative in the company, and I was chomping at the bit to get my hands on one of the organization's key accounts. Now, this was a big company, a firm that was already buying from us and that handled a large volume of financial trade transactions every day. One day, my wish became reality; I was given responsibility for this key account, which had just purchased 200 units of our product. Why did this great gift come my way? Because the account manager had just been promoted! I couldn't believe my luck. I had been at the right place at the right time. Times were good!

Or so I thought.

I can still recall walking eagerly into the office of my new contact, the vice president of facilities. I had a big smile on my face, and I was confident that this initial meeting was going to go wonderfully. Before I stepped in the door, the vice president's assistant stopped me and asked, "Do you really want to go in there?"

I asked him somewhat nervously what he meant. The assistant informed me that there had been had been nothing but problems with our units for the past week and that his boss was extremely upset.

And indeed he was. The moment I walked in, this 6'4" former Army colonel simply pointed at me and said that he did not want to hear a peep out of me. I felt like the Cowardly Lion from *The Wizard of Oz,* desperately searching for some semblance of courage, but all I could hear was a little voice inside chanting, "I want to go home!" My "meeting" lasted all of two minutes. The vice president did all the talking; he didn't want to hear anything that I had to say.

All he cared to discuss was the massive liability and regulatory risk his firm was facing because the units that we had sold to them were not synching up properly with each other. The vice president informed me that I had exactly two weeks to fix the problem. If I didn't, we were history at his company. Can you imagine how I felt? After only two days of being responsible for the kind of big client I had been dreaming about for months, I was already well on my way to losing the account!

I went back to my office to talk to the service manager about the train-wreck of a meeting from which I'd just emerged. He knew, as I expected he might, that there was big trouble afoot. What I didn't expect, however, was that he would not even want to see me. That's how bad *his* day was going.

I managed to talk my way into his office. He knew why I was there, and he didn't really want to hear what I had to say. Once I'd gotten him to take a deep breath, I said, as calmly as I possibly could, "We need to fix this."

The manager informed me that his service techs had already changed the motors in all the units and that he had no idea what else to do. He told me that this customer had been totally uncooperative and that he had too many customers to take care of and not enough bodies to take care of them with. He also let me know, in so many words, that I would just have to find some way to finesse this problem. He'd done his best. He was burned out. He only had so many hours in the day. (He went on like that for a while.)

When I heard his responses, my initial instinct was to start yelling. Didn't he get it? Wasn't the customer supposed to come first? What was he talking about, only so many hours in the day? This was a big customer!

I was about to give him a piece of my mind when I realized that I was probably better off shutting up and letting him continue to vent. I had to let him share his frustrations if I was going to succeed in finding a bridge that would solve our shared problem. For just a moment, I tried to see things from his perspective.

The service manager had his own quota. He had a profit and loss target that he had to meet, and a lot of other standards that I knew absolutely nothing about. He really was understaffed, and he couldn't let one account throw his entire operation off-kilter. He had already invested significant resources into solving this dilemma, and he felt the he had gone far above and beyond the call of duty. He was mystified, and he honestly didn't know what to do next.

In an attempt to empathize with his situation, I told the manager, "You sound like you've been given way too much to do."

He replied, "You're absolutely right. Why they think I can work miracles on this budget, and with this level of staffing, I will never know." This was a perspective that was important to him that I hear. He needed to process that emotionally, and he needed to be sure that I was processing it, too.

There was a pause during which I let him collect himself. Once he did, we were back at square one together. The customer was still unhappy, and we still had to do something. But we were connected in a way in which we hadn't been before.

I asked him whether our people used a logging system to identify exactly which units were having the problems. He told me that his team did not have time to keep a log. Therefore, they had no idea which units were failing. This was clearly a problem, and it was part of the reason why my client was operating under the assumption that there was a flaw with every single unit: He didn't have any evidence to the contrary.

I asked the service manager whether we could help each other out. If I created the log, and got my contact's assistant to hold on to it, would he simply ask his people to jot down the serial numbers of the machines they were working on so we could start to get some idea of which units were breaking?

It seems like a logical solution, doesn't it? Why wouldn't the service manager have done something like this from the beginning?[1] The answer is that he was overworked and operating from his own mindset; he simply did not see tracking down the units that were failing as a step that might solve the issue that we were having. This problem was only one of a hundred that he had on his desk, whereas it was the biggest problem that I was facing.

The service manager agreed to my idea for a couple of reasons: It didn't actually require him to put anything new on his to-do list, and it sounded like it might eventually take a problem off his list. That was what he wanted to hear. I now had an internal ally with whom I could work.

After about a week or so, the manager and I revisited the problem and reviewed the log together. Upon doing so, we realized that only 20 percent of the units were failing. Armed with that information, I asked the service manager how we could figure out how to fix those specific units. Since I was now his ally—someone who understood his position—he was now more inclined to work with me to try to figure this out. There was also a professional engineering challenge to all of this, which I think he might have appreciated: If he'd swapped out the motors on all the units, and some—but not all—were still failing, that meant that there was another problem that was common to the units that had failed. After our talk, he was now a little curious about what that problem could be.

While the service manager was investigating that particular issue, I went back to the vice president at the financial services company to let him know what I'd found out and share my plan. The failure rate was 20 percent, not 100 percent as he'd thought at first. I assured him that I

---

[1] I should say that, today, the concept of asking for a serial number is standard operating procedure on both sides at the start of a service call in this industry. In the early 1980s, however, people didn't always follow this procedure. Also, to be fair to my service manager, I want to emphasize here that he had already replaced all the motors in all of the units, and had every reason to expect that the problem should have been resolved by this step.

was fully aware that the rate was still too high and that my immediate goal was to get the problem down to a manageable 10 perent or less. But either way—whether the failure rate was 20 percent or 10 percent—I recommended that he buy 20 spares, so that when a unit went down, he could replace the unit immediately. That way, he could avoid any problems with synchronization, keep from having interruptions in his trading operations, and get back on track.

The vice president was a little calmer this time, because he knew we were taking steps to fix the situation. By the end of the short meeting, he agreed with my assessment and the need to buy the spares. He knew this recommendation was not made to simply sell a couple of more units. At this point, he seemed to feel that I was acting as a trusted advisor on his behalf, and he agreed with my recommendations.

Our company eventually used this spare system to win the day. We reduced the failure rate to an acceptable 5 percent, made it easy to swap in new units, and repaired the relationship with our customer, who ended up expanding its operations and awarding us another deal for 1,000 units. During this period, by the way, the vice president, invited me in to the project meetings. This was crucial, because some of the players involved wanted to bring in my competition. Because I had effectively positioned myself as a trusted advisor to the vice president, he created the opportunity for me to deal with my detractors directly ... and win them over.

This result could never have happened if I'd simply started yelling at my service manager and started listing to him all the ways in which he had let me down. Sure I could have told the service manager that I was losing sleep as a result of the predicament or having problems in other areas of my job as a result of the stress that he was putting me through. But what would that have accomplished?

When you have an internal problem at your organization—when somebody overlooks something or misses a deadline that affects your world—getting agitated and throwing a temper tantrum is the least constructive way to solve the problem. Yelling doesn't turn you into an ally for that person. It turns you into someone to avoid.

In many of my seminars and coaching programs, I oversee role-plays where I challenge sales executives to find ways to improve their interaction with real-life colleagues. This topic—poor communication between sales executives and those with whom they work—is often a major challenge within the organization, and the role-plays sometimes uncover some long-simmering conflicts and misunderstandings. Most of these clashes stem from the widely held perception among non-sales employees that sales executives consider their own issues to be more pressing than everyone else's. You know what? They're right.

While it's true that "nothing happens until somebody sells something," it's also true that nothing happens after you sell something until you can get someone inside your organization to help you deliver on your promises. And while all members of the organization should ideally operate from a sales mind set, that does not mean that everyone is automatically motivated to support you at the levels you feel that you deserve. They will only become motivated to help you when they feel certain that you care about their interests. Your colleagues will first tend to take on actions that will help them to succeed in their roles. Why not show them how what you want to do connects to helping them succeed?

Think back to the service manager who helped me solve a problem with my most important client. When did he start buying into the idea of working with me? The moment that I began to empathize with him, of course, Doesn't that approach make a lot more sense than immediately launching into combat mode by reciting a long list of the various ways in which he and his people had let me and the company down? I could have completed that performance by raising the issue to a higher level. What would have happened if we'd decided to play that game? Well, his boss would have defended his actions, just as my vice president would have defended mine. Time would have been wasted; bridges would have been burned. And the customer would have suffered.

I didn't have time for any of that. I needed an ally. So I decided to have a different kind of conversation.

Why go through all of the pain and trauma of complaining about each other—and telling on your coworkers—when you can simply take responsibility for building the alliances you need to succeed? That is what sales leaders do. They solve problems and move on!

Winning the War, Not the Battle

Building alliances—within your company or anywhere else— inevitably involves conflict resolution. When you find yourself in the middle of a dispute, remember this simple rule: You can win the battle or the war; the choice is yours.

The Leader's Advantage

"The quickest way to kindle a fire is to rub two opposing opinions together."—Anonymous

---

Many people get trapped in the emotion of the conflict and do whatever they can to win a given battle . . . even if that means losing the war. In this situation, our emotions can be our own worst enemy.

The first thing you must do when you're facing any kind of discord is to recognize the other person's pain. That doesn't mean that your organization has to assume formal responsibility for the thing your prospect or customer identifies as the source of the complaint, but you can recognize and try to empathize with the problems that other people are experiencing. And if you aspire to become a sales leader, you should know that you will have to become very good at talking about other people's problems—from their point of view.

In fact, you will have to do even more than that. To succeed as a leader in any field that involves conflict resolution—such as sales—you must become familiar with four basic psychological processes of human interaction: acknowledgement, empathy, solution, and commitment.

- *Acknowledge* the other person's pain,
- *Empathize* with his or her issues and concerns,
- Provide *solutions* to eliminate the pain, and
- Make a *commitment* on how to move forward.

Many people try to circumvent this process by eliminating the initial steps of acknowledgement and empathy. But these two processes are essential if you expect the other party to hear and buy into your proposed solution. As the leader, you must first acknowledge and empathize with those whom you are hoping to lead. We often mistakenly attempt to present a solution without even bothering to hear the other party's issues. Even if your solution is perfect, which—let's be honest—it probably isn't, your ideas will land on deaf ears. The person to whom you are offering advice won't process anything you're saying because his anger will be building. All he will be able to focus on is the fact you do not understand what he is going through. Your solution cannot be valid in his world.

Resolving conflict requires enhancing your ability to influence others by listening. To gain influence, you need to convince the other side that you truly understand what is going on. Only then can you suggest a solution. Skipping the first step of understanding minimizes the value of your solution and dramatically reduces the chance that it will be accepted.

Suppose that I had cut off all conversation with that service manager, made no attempt to listen to him, and simply demanded that he start keeping proper logs on his own equipment. Perhaps he would have told me he would do so in order to placate me, even if he had no intention of keeping his word. Or, perhaps he would have gotten testy and told me where I could go. How would most people respond after being reprimanded for screwing up—by a *salesperson*? Whatever he chose to do, there would have been very little chance that he would actually place that item on the top of his to-do list. Why? He had no reason to follow through for me. I was not yet his ally!

If you're like most salespeople, you might be wondering how you can go about building the alliances you need. Consider the following list of simple steps you can take to build stronger alliances with internal allies and improve your conflict resolution skills.

Seven Steps for Conflict Resolution and Building Internal Alliances

1. Do not assign blame or wrongdoing on either side.
2. Strip away the emotion and look for a way to allow everyone to win.
3. Put your own needs to the side, and try to understand the issues facing the person you're talking to.
4. Find out what's important to the other person.
5. Find a middle ground that will enable both sides to align their purposes.
6. Try to engage the other person in identifying a solution along with you. If the person helps to craft the solution, he or she will be more motivated to support it.
7. Secure agreement on a path forward complete with actions, timelines, and accountabilities.

Building Customer Alliances

Just as you need to build alliances internally, you must form relationships with customers and clients. As a general rule, salespeople often limit their interactions to a single key point of contact at a customer organization. They reject concepts such as calling high (meaning, say, reaching out to the C suite of executives) or calling wide (meaning reaching out to people who work in multiple departments). This tendency is usually not simple rejection, but rather a reflection of a need to keep within one's comfort zone. Unfortunately, remaining within your comfort zone will not allow you to achieve exponential success. You need to expand your alliances to gain access to new opportunities, protect existing opportunities, and increase your value to the buying organization.

There are three critical customer mindsets a salesperson encounters when it comes to building alliances on the buyer's side.

1. *The Comparative Mindset*—This mindset guides an individual or group who is tasked with comparing your products and services with those of your competitors. They can evaluate what you offer on price, quality, or design, and they can compare it based on operational issues. Build alliances with them that help them see how your overall value exceeds that of the competition.
2. *The Implementer Mindset*—These are the people who are actually going to be using the product. Typically, they are concerned with how your products and services are going to make their lives easier. While they are extremely unlikely to make the decision alone, their support for any initiative is critical. Build alliances with them based on making their lives easier.
3. *The Decision-Making Mindset*—Members of this group have to sign off on whether or not your products or services are actually

being purchased. In many cases, even though these individuals may never use your products or services, they still have to approve the transactions. They are concerned with one thing only: the outcome of their decision. Will the decision make them look competent or inept? How is this decision going to benefit the enterprise or organization? Build alliances with them based on potentially helpful outcomes that will benefit the organization as a whole—and make them look like a hero to the rest of the company in the process.

If you are selling products to a small company that only houses a couple of people on site in the office, there is a very good chance that one person may represent all three mindsets. But whether a single person or several people are signing off on the deal, you will need to be ready to *address* all three mindsets. Ignoring any one mindset will inevitably limit the perceived value of your solution.

For instance, if you are selling a service to a married couple, one of the two individuals is probably responsible for comparing (comparative mindset) your offering against the competition. One of the two will probably be the one using the service (that's the implementer mindset), and one of the two may have more say in the matter about whether and when to get started (that's the decision-making mindset). But which member of the couple will make which decisions? Do you have some idea of who fits where? If not, how can you possibly expect to build an alliance with this couple? If you don't have some sense of which mindset(s) each person occupies, you won't attract many allies—because the agendas in the three cases are so very different.

A few years ago, a manufacturer with whom I had been working asked me for some advice on a negotiation. The company had been supplying their product to an equipment manufacturer, and the annual contract was about to expire. Their customer's vice president of purchasing was throwing nothing but hardball tactics at them. My client was told that another vendor was already certified and that if they did not deliver at a certain price, they were sure to lose the business.

My client was panicking; my first step was to calm him down and attempt to remove the emotional component of his reaction. I learned that it had been a while since the sales team had visited this customer's manufacturing plants, so I suggested that we send the sales people out to the plants to talk to the plant managers, the line operators, and anyone else we could track down. Our goal was to converse with all of the mindsets that we could and find out what we could uncover.

Upon entering the premises on his visit to the customer's plant, one of the salespeople promptly tripped over a box in the entrance way. A worker came running to his aide and asked if he was all right. The salesperson said that he was fine and inquired about the contents of the box. The answer came back: "Nothing but a lousy, low-quality product that management wants us to use." It turned out to be the competitor's product that had supposedly been certified!

When we made this discovery, who do you think had the upper hand in the negotiation? We did! Identifying the fact that our competitor was delivering low-quality product helped us to focus our message to three different constituencies of customers. The low-quality product made life more difficult for the people on the front lines who actually had to use it. The inferior nature of the competitor's merchandise helped us to make our comparative case with the people who were analyzing us against the competition, allowing us to make an apples-to-apples comparison. We knew, too, that we could make it easier for the people in the decision-making mindset to look like heroes by picking our company, which is exactly what ended up happening.

We never used what we had found out in our pitch in any overt way. We just took the intelligence we had gathered from end-users to confirm what we already expected: that we were not as far behind the eight ball as the customer had led us to believe during these negotiations. We now knew for certain that we were in the driver's seat in terms of quality, and that changed our whole view on how to proceed with the negotiation. If we had told our customer that we knew the competitor was having quality issues, the customer could very possibly have gone into a defensive posture—perhaps by contradicting us or doing something else to aid our competitor and save face. This isn't what we wanted; we wanted to solidify our own position as an ally for this client, and we managed to do just that.

The Leader's Advantage

Not everyone can say "yes" and make a sale happen . . . but just about everyone can say "no" and make a sale more unlikely. A sales leader knows the final decision maker will rarely override the majority.

A Fourth Mindset

We've looked at three critical mindset constituencies within the buying organization. There is one other mindset we need to talk about: the Coaching Mindset. The coach may be the CEO, the executive assistant of the CEO, or the vice president of sales; he or she also may represent any other position in the organization. The coach may have some other formal role or title that seems to have nothing whatsoever to do with the product or service you are selling; yet this person emerges as a critical ally for you and your organization because he or she realizes the potential of your offering for the organization. This person also knows the ins and outs of how buying decisions are made in the organization.

You should not expect a coach to materialize out of nowhere or to volunteer information. You should expect a coach to respond positively when you ask courteously "How things operate around here." Take good notes when you get an answer that connects to your world. Figure out this person's long-term goals, and prove that you and your product/service are committed to supporting those goals. Find a way to build an alliance with this coach based on common interests.

In most sales scenarios—and in *all* situations where the sale affects more than one person or department—there is likely to be at least one informed person who can act as the coach. This coach knows how to get things done in a way that is ethical, legal, effective, and in the best interests of his or her organization. Your goal is to make sure this person is identified and enrolled on your behalf. Any help you can get in guiding the turbulent waters of a purchasing decision will be vital.

Once you've identified your coach, the rules are simple: follow his or her lead.

Your mission is to work with the coach to make sure that when the roll call is taken, the "no" votes are in the minority and the "yes" votes prevail. It's actually very rare for the final decision maker to force their own preference on the people who have to carry out the game plan. The final decision maker's role is more likely to be that of a tie-breaker; in the end, it's his or her people who have to produce the results. This means that you have to have the right constituency on your side.

The method is simple: work with the coach to learn as much as you legally can about who's who, what's what, and what the priorities are. That's the only way to create a coalition of the willing that includes not just the formal decision maker, but also the various team members who will have to use, evaluate, and/or implement what you sell. Once you have this coalition, you are no longer as vulnerable to sudden, unforeseen disasters that you should have—and could have—foreseen (such as the sudden departure of a decision maker who represents your sole contact within the organization).

You May Need More Than One Coach

Several years ago, following a keynote address that I gave at a North America sales meeting in Las Vegas for a major manufacturing firm, the North American business operations manager approached me about doing an eight-city tour to connect with a broader audience in his organization. Before getting approval for this tour, we had to convince the vice president of sales that this would be a valuable investment. The business operations manager set up an all-day meeting between the vice president, his direct reports, and me.

At the beginning of the meeting, I started to review my capabilities. One of the phrases that I frequently used to explain my approach was "value-add selling." Immediately, the vice president stopped me and asked the team, "If he talks about value-add selling, what is the sales force going to do?" His managers all said the sales force would revolt.

I went on to the next phrase, "key account selling," and got the same kind of response. After three of these exchanges I gave up and told the vice president that I was confused. He wanted me to educate his salespeople on skills that would make them more successful, yet he and his team were rejecting the very topics that would do that. I asked him to help me out.

As it turned out, a thorough grounding in value-add selling was exactly what his team needed from our eight-city tour. The problem was that if I used that particular terminology—or anything connected to it—the salespeople would in fact revolt! They had received similarly named training in the past and had never really implemented it. The terms would set off the alarms with the sales force: "Here it comes again—the flavor of the month!"

This was a discussion that my coach—the business operations manager—knew that I had to have face-to-face with the vice president and his team. That's why he'd arranged the meeting. My task during that meeting was twofold. I had to (a) position the upcoming tour as a process for helping the sales force with its current challenges, which meant avoiding terminology that might bring on the apathy (or wrath) of the sales force, and (b) make a persuasive commitment to stand by my training, and reinforce it, until it became standard operating procedure within this company.

During that meeting, the vice president became another coach for me, specifically on how we needed to present this program and gain buy-in throughout the organization. I never would have gotten the meeting with the vice president of sales without my first coach at that company, and I never would have closed the deal without my second coach! The moral: Don't rely on one contact... and keep looking for new coaches.

If you only have one contact in the organization, you deserve whatever happens to you when that person leaves, gets hit by a bus, or (even worse) starts taking calls from the competition!

Advocate Alliances

Mark LeBlanc, author of the great book *Growing Your Business,* advocates what he calls a "Target 25 Advocate Strategy." Mark's advice is to build a list of 25 prominent people within your industry who can be the source of referrals for the future, if you stay in touch with them over time. These people might be key influencers in your market, or existing customers with whom you want to expand your business relationship. The idea is that these are long-term advocates who buy into the value of your products and services.

How should you stay in touch with these people? That's really up to you. You can mail or e-mail articles on a regular basis; you can forward a book that you've found to be valuable, with a particular section highlighted; you can send along some kind of branded promotional item. The point is to stay in touch, and to include a brief, *personalized* message with each touch.

The key to making this strategy work is having the right people on the list and communicating with them consistently. The list will change as some names come off and others are added. You cannot expect to build your sales or business without having heroes or advocates who support your cause. This third level of alliance-building is more long term in nature than the internal kind or the customer-based kind, but it is just as essential to the generation of referrals and the creation of long-term strategic alliances.

Social Networking and Alliance-Building

What are you looking to do when you build a new alliance? Basically, you're trying to get into someone's office, find the decision makers, turn cold calls into warm calls, and expand your network. Your ability to network on a social basis is going to come into play here.

You won't be surprised to learn that a large proportion of social networking and initial contact today takes place online. Many salespeople have great-looking web sites and/or contact pages on their company's web site, but they have not taken full advantage of the online social media resources that can help drive qualified traffic to those sites. These sites are an essential business tool, not just a recreational channel. Make sure you have a business presence on the Internet because your competition certainly does.

There are several networking communities on the Internet that can help you gain exposure. Some are clearly business-related, such as LinkedIn, Ecademy and Plaxo. Others, like Facebook and MySpace, are more socially oriented. However, important introductions and contacts can come from any of these sites. Follow the rules of the site and put in a little bit of time each month on the sites you join.

For example, LinkedIn is a business networking site that follows the premise you are only a few "degrees of separation" away from an introduction to more people than you could ever imagine possible.

As of this writing, I have 218 connections in my list. These are people I have personally invited to join my network. According to LinkedIn, I have access to 1,904,600 people through those 218 contacts. Let's suppose you are a direct connection of mine. A person I want to meet is connected to someone who is connected to you. That's three degrees—from me to you (one) to your connection (two) to the person I want to meet (three).

There was a particular executive I have been trying to reach for months, and it turns out he was connected to one of my 218 connections. Through one of our common contacts, I got in touch with him! Then there was a new prospect who recently contacted me; he found my profile through a mutual connection on LinkedIn as well.

Similar possibilities abound at the web sites Ecademy (which offers "online networking for business, offline networking events, and global networking groups") and Plaxo (which helps you "stay in touch with people you care about"). What's really interesting—as you will learn for yourself when you become a student of these sites—is how many key decision makers have entries on one, two, or all three sites! Check for yourself and then find a way to reach out.

Build "End to End" Alliances

How does an airline service the global market if it does not physically fly to every corner of the Earth? By building alliances! These connections allow the airlines to deliver solutions to their customers that would have been too costly to offer on their own.

Executive Vice President of Marketing at Continental Airlines Jim Compton points out that when it comes to partnerships between major carriers "size does matter." Airlines are relying increasingly on long-term business alliances with companies they used to consider competitors. Why? Because these connections help the airlines to grow revenue streams while simultaneously controlling costs.

Business alliances are an alternative to mergers—something that Continental had initially considered but ultimately avoided due to the current market environment. The company looked closely at the possibility of merging with United Airlines in 2008 to help combat the higher costs facing the industry and the mergers announced by other airlines. However, Continental made the strategic decision to stay independent, yet enhance its alliance by changing partners and joining United Airlines in the StarAlliance. This allowed Continental to provide destinations—and rewards points—under its own brand that it otherwise could not have offered its customers. Notice what has happened here: Continental has tapped into a powerful global network and has secured compelling brand advantages in a tough marketplace by leveraging the capacities of other allied companies that do what they themselves don't do.

Could your organization build strategic alliances like that?

The sales lesson here is a significant one: Strategic alliances help you win credit for all aspects of the solution you provide, even when a partner is taking responsibility for delivering on a given commitment you pass along. Here's my question for you: What creative, strategically driven organizational and personal alliances can you create or help to create that will help you to deliver and win credit for results that your partners convey on your behalf?

Compton draws a parallel between his airline's strategy for building alliances and the sales leader's strategy for keeping customers happy with good business connections. Continental has what it calls an "End to End" strategy for establishing alliances with its passengers. If, for instance, an executive wants to fly Continental from Newark to Thailand, Continental can only get that executive as far as Japan. However, one of Continental's network partners can fly that passenger to his final destination of Thailand. The "End to End" principle allows Continental to use its coalition of partners to fly passengers to destinations that their own routes don't include—while the customer still thinks of the journey as a Continental flight!

How does this method relate to sales? Well, consider this: When Tim Seale of Timber Trading hired me to develop a custom selling process for his newly developed Clear Solutions™ program; we discovered that we needed to engage a marketing company to help create and communicate the message. I called upon an alliance that I had with a top-notch marketing organization, and that company helped to make the rollout a big success. Why did Tim trust my recommendation about a marketing company? Because I had earned Tim's trust, and he knew that I would be working with the marketing company to ensure that their work supported our previous efforts. This is a classic example of end-to-end alliance building. The client was relying on me to call on my alliances, bring someone of quality in, and provide a solution. Ultimately, this alliance allowed me to enhance my company's value and generate a higher level of success for the client.

Your Chapter Six Commitment

Use the Commitment Sheet that follows to answer these questions:

Are your alliances strong enough to get you to where you want to be one year from now?

What are you willing to do differently in terms of building and strengthening alliances to expand your business?

When will you do that?

With whom should you be building new alliances in:

- Your company?
- Your customer's organization?
- Your network of providers of services that can enhance your value?
- Your network of influencers who can introduce you to new prospects?

COMMITMENT!

(Pronunciation: ko-'mit-mint, Function: noun, Definition: a: an agreement or pledge to do something in the future; b: something pledged c: the state or an instance of being obligated or emotionally impelled, a commitment to a cause)

For more of these sample sheets go to http://www.leadsellorgetoutoftheway.com.

Figure 6.1   Commitment Sheet

7 | Asking Good Questions

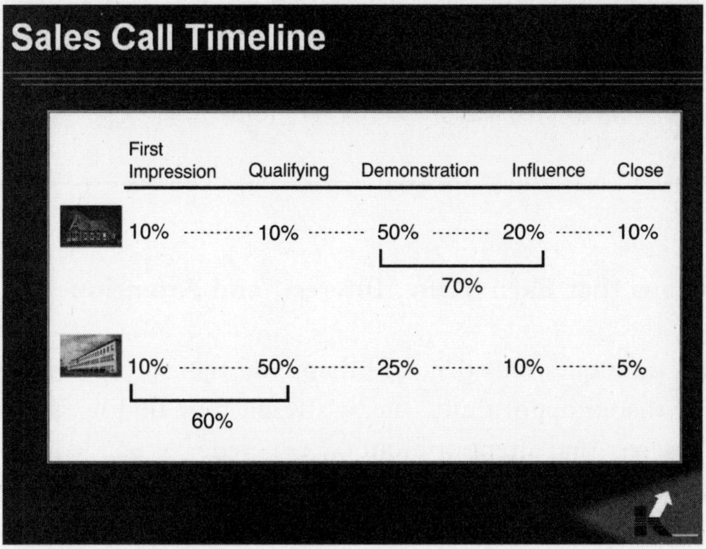

Figure 7.1

There are sales leaders ... and there are followers who happen to sell for a living. The quality of the questions we ask is what drives the customer's perception about which category we occupy.

This chapter takes us to the qualifying stage of the Sales Call Timeline. Bear in mind that that the more time you spend in this stage, the less time you'll need to spend presenting your solutions. Although you're exerting more effort during the beginning of the relationship and the sales call asking questions, the overall cycle time will be reduced. Why? Because you'll spend less time going back and forth, getting feedback on your presentation and making course corrections. By doing what leaders do—asking the *right* questions up front—you will develop a customized solution that is focused like a laser beam, which is a solution that your prospect perceives as highly valuable.

The Leader's Wisdom

"Leadership: the art of getting someone else to do something that you want done because he wants to do it."—Dwight D. Eisenhower

Questions that Earn Time, Interest, and Attention

Leaders pose questions that lead them and their prospects toward a zone of shared opportunity, and as a result they find it easy to earn time, interest, and attention from other people.

All too often, salespeople ask questions that don't support this critical goal, particularly when they are initiating contact with a new potential client. The first few moments that you share with a prospective ally will usually determine whether that person perceives you as a leader—as someone who is willing and able to take action in a bold way on shared opportunities. Sales leaders know how important those first few moments are, and accordingly they choose their questions—particularly their early questions—with great care.

How Much Thought Do You Give to Your Questions?

Many salespeople do not spend enough time considering the questions that they pose to potential customers. They simply launch into task mode, asking a few perfunctory questions that are supposedly geared toward making the sale. Some salespeople don't even ask questions at all, but immediately go into a show-and-tell routine about a certain feature that they (not the client) find particularly interesting.

That's very different from what leaders do. Leaders begin by asking questions in purpose mode. You will never witness a true sales leader inquiring about what product or service another person is currently using at the very beginning of a relationship. Sales leaders will never try to sell a feature that they have no reason to believe will be perceived as valuable to an individual whom they've just met a moment before. Although these are common sales openings, they're not the ways that leaders build relationships.

Are You Opening with the Questions a Leader Would Ask?

If I were to call you on the phone in an effort to sell you on my company's bundled Internet, long-distance, and television service, and if my very first question was "What communications provider are you currently using?" how would you answer?

In all likelihood, you'd move into defense mode. You'd get ready for yet another verbal wrestling match with yet another pushy, self-absorbed salesperson. You might even think, "Wait a minute. I don't even know you. I didn't ask for this call. I'm not having any problems with my communications provider. Why should I let you steal my precious time? So I can give you an in-depth briefing about my communications vendor? How absurd is that?" And that's only if you even bothered to participate in the call long enough to start such an internal monologue. It's far more likely that you would simply hang up!

We wonder why prospects tune out salespeople. It's because salespeople rarely stop to think about the emotional reactions they elicit in potential clients. We push for a full history of what's happened and when, and we ignore what the prospect is thinking when we continue to push incessantly: "Hey, it's not my job to give you an education about my company. Who are you, anyway, and why does it even make sense for me to have this conversation with you? What's in it for me?"

That kind of internal monologue is definitely *not* what you want to initiate as you start your relationship. In my experience, many decision makers—and most high-level senior executives—are extremely skittish about releasing information about their current operations at the outset of a relationship with a new salesperson. And why shouldn't they be? Salespeople who probe for information, much of it clearly proprietary, before they've given the prospect any reason to provide that information only end up aggravating people. Why would you want to aggravate someone you're trying to sell to?

Your prospects will give you reliable information only when they have established a comfort zone with you, only when they are convinced that the information will be treated with respect and discretion, and only when they are confident that sharing the information has a realistic chance of bringing them closer to realizing some important goal of their own.

Now consider this: At some point, when you were faced with a pushy salesperson, did you ever decide that it made sense to play along and see what kind of information you could get that might make it a little bit easier for you to negotiate a better deal from your current supplier? We salespeople often make a big show out of resenting this, but don't we do it ourselves, as customers? And isn't this betrayal we're so used to complaining about the result of the lousy questions with which we've used to open the relationship?

> ### The Leader's Advantage
>
> You cannot expect people to tell you what is happening in their world, or what they want to accomplish in their companies and their careers, simply because you give them an instant recommendation based on ... nothing. No bonding and rapport. No past experience. No clear, shared zones of opportunity. Just your own assertion that what you are selling would work for them, too. That's not how leaders sell!

If we'd asked better questions—questions that positioned us as leaders who were genuinely interested in identifying areas of mutual opportunity—do you think our prospects would take the trouble to play that game? We got those answers, wasted our time, and gave away our information and strategies to the competition because we used questions that were important to us but not the customer. Nine times out of ten, what we want to know is some variation on "What are you using right now?" And beginning a business relationship by grilling the prospect about their current product or service—with or without some supposedly attention-getting icebreaker session up front—is a great way to position yourself as a follower, rather than a leader.

Opening questions like these are known as status-based questions. They focus on what the prospect is currently doing—how he or she is currently handling things. These are, in essence, completely ineffective opening questions. Leaders do not open the business phase of any discussion by asking status-based questions.

Why not? Well, for one thing, those are precisely the kinds of questions that *followers who happen to sell for a living* ask, and leaders are in no hurry to be confused with those people. For another thing, these questions don't tell the leader anything about what the person is striving for in life—either on the job or off. Consequently, they don't get the leader any closer to General Eisenhower's goal of "getting someone else to do what you want to do ... because he wants to do it." Lastly, and most important, status-based questions reduce the size of the playing field. These questions inevitably revolve around a few narrowly defined issues, products, or services. Status-based questions are inherently commodity driven; they pit one product or service against another and limit your value by forcing you to play the competition's game. Status-based questions prevent you from uncovering the higher-level issues that could enable you to sell more to the customer and increase the perceived value of your overall solution. You always want to change the game and elevate yourself above the competition, and status-based questions don't allow you to do that at the beginning of the relationship.

The Leader's Advantage

Status-based questions have their place, but they won't help you establish yourself as a leader at the beginning of the discussion!

Here are some additional examples of status-based questions that make terrible opening questions:

- Who do you buy your copiers from now?
- What stocks and mutual funds are you currently investing in?
- How do you like your current vendor?

- Is everything going okay with your current vendor? (This is a particularly stupid opening question, because unless there is a full-scale disaster in process with the current vendor, you will always get a "yes" answer to this. And if there *is* a disaster in process, the prospect may be too distracted by it to focus fully on you!)

So, how *does* a leader open the conversation with a potential new ally? They begin by asking issues-based questions.

Issues-Based Questions

Issues-based questions are aimed at finding out where the other person is trying to go. They revolve around fears, needs, and desires. They address the gaps that the customer is looking to close *now*, gaps that are somehow preventing this person from achieving goals, removing pain, or eradicating obstacles to some kind of competitive advantage. Issues-based questions may also focus on what's preventing our allies from experiencing the pleasurable encounters and outcomes that they're truly seeking.

Here are some examples of good issues-based questions:

- Describe the three biggest challenges that your company is facing right now in reaching its business goals.
- What do you want your customers to think of when they hear your company's name?
- Please describe the top three initiatives for which you're personally responsible.
- Please describe the three outcomes you're most interested in bringing about as a result of your outsourcing initiative.

- What do you want to see happening differently in your company six months from now?
- What are the three things you want to do most when you retire?

The higher up the organizational ladder you go, the more excited people will get about answering these kinds of questions.

Leaders know that people love talking about their goals. That's why they focus on issues-based questions first, rather than status-based questions.

This is a principle as reliable as any law of physics. People will tend to open up more quickly with you when you ask about where they're trying to go with their business and personal goals than they will when you ask about what product, service, or vendor they're using.

The Leader's Advantage

Do what the leaders do: ask issues-based questions at the beginning of any business relationship.

Are You a Trusted Advisor?

A few years ago, a financial services organization hired my firm to come in and examine its sales training program. After carefully scrutinizing the program, I realized that their financial advisors were being encouraged to spend a great deal of their time in the early part of an initial meeting on small talk that was supposed to help them build up relationships with decision makers.

The financial advisors were supposed to establish rapport with their prospects by complimenting the pictures of family members on the person's desk or asking about the weather. They were easing into the questioning phase of the discussion with some classic—and, to the prospects, all-too-familiar—meet-and-greet maneuvers.

If you were in a meeting with the President of the United States—or any other top-tier leader you care to name—how much time do you think you would spend on icebreakers at the beginning of the meeting? Little time or no time at all, right? Today, none of us have time for extended small talk. All of us would prefer, if at all possible, to be treated like the President.

In this case, these financial advisors were not treating their prospects and customers as though they were V.I.P.s with valuable, limited time. Instead, they were unwittingly using vast amounts of small talk in a way that actually built up walls between themselves and their prospects. It's hard to make the case that you're an important professional resource when you're sending this message: "I'm really uncomfortable about getting to the point I want to make, so let's talk about the ballgame." You will never, ever see a true leader selling in this way.

Of course, you need to build relationships. Of course, you must establish rapport. Each person has his or her own style.

The problem arises when we try to use small talk as a replacement for asking powerful questions. By asking great issues-based questions early on in the discussion, you will find that you're actually able to build a much stronger connection—at a faster rate of speed—than you are with small talk . . . That's because issues-based questions are about your customers and their concerns, not you! Yes, you should use your personal style to establish rapport . . . , but do so in short order, and make sure that you begin posing value-generating questions as soon as possible.

This was the challenge facing the financial advisors with whom I was working. They weren't getting to their value-generating questions quickly enough! I assured management that two things would happen as a result of their team's implementing the questioning sequence I was about to build into their sales process. First, the financial advisors would reduce the total number of "touches" necessary to close a new client, and second, they would acquire a significant amount of additional assets to manage, thereby increasing their earnings.

I knew that the team would be able to deliver these outcomes if they started launching their business relationships in the same way that leaders do. And they did. The team was able change the way they began their conversations—and ultimately delivered on both of the outcomes I had promised management. After they introduced themselves, shook hands, and offered their Resource Proclamation, the advisors moved directly to an issues-based question that focused on the prospect's needs, fears, or desires.

So after the financial advisor had introduced herself, engaged the client in a very short period of small talk, and presented her Resource Proclamation, she would ask, "Would you mind if I asked you an important question?" Most of her prospects would tell her to go ahead and ask. The advisor would then respond by saying something like this: "Tell me something: What would you say are the three most important things you want your investments to accomplish for you?" (Notice how different that question is from, "What firm are you using now, and what kind of investments have you been making?")

Something very interesting happens once get you get into the habit of asking potential clients an issues-based question at the outset of the relationship. The person's whole physical posture changes; his or her facial expressions change. In fact, we actually tested this approach by videotaping prospects during the early phase of the sale. (These prospects agreed to be part of a focus group study.) The way that these prospects reacted to salespeople who opened up the meeting in the way I'm describing was quite dramatic. The potential client's eyes would shift upward, and he or she would immediately go into a thinking posture, as opposed to the defensive, neutral, poker-faced style of communication that's so common among prospects taking part in early sales calls.

The Leader's Advantage

When you open up the relationship as a leader does—that is, when you keep the pleasantries short and move briskly to an important issues-based question—the prospect actually brings the walls down for you.

Prospects start talking about what they want to do and say things like, "Oh, I would like to be able to retire by such-and-such a year, and this is what I want my retirement to look like"; or "I want my kids to be able to go to college without taking out loans"; or "I want my parents to be well taken care of when they need help."

That's what issues-based questions do for leaders: They bring down walls, identify zones of shared opportunity, and get people talking. It's amazing how much more quickly you can uncover crucial information with these kinds of questions. That's why leaders almost always lead the discussion with issues-based questions ... and why you should do the same, if you plan to sell (and influence) like a leader.

Leaders Use This Stuff—Because It Works!

As you become more familiar with the idea of leading your discussions by asking issues-based questions, you will see for yourself that this really is the best way to begin conversations with prospects—and everyone else who has a stake in your company's process.

These kinds of questions allow you to focus on the one underlying question that just about everyone loves to answer in depth: "Where

---

A Word about "Selling" . . .

In some industries, the words "sell" and "selling" are taboo. For example, members of the financial services sector prefer that their rainmakers act as "consultants." They shy away from the word "sell" because of their sensitivity to being perceived as being too pushy.

Please, if you fall into this category, do not put this book down! It is meant for you! Simply replace the word "sell" with "advise," "consult," or any word your particular field deems appropriate. Whatever industry you are in, we are talking about being a trusted advisor who asks the right questions.

The last thing I want you to do is sell something someone does not need nor want. That is self-serving, unethical, and transactional. Asking issues-based questions that uncover the most important objectives, however, is something trusted advisors can do and should do, regularly, as a matter of professional responsibility!

---

are you trying to go?" Ultimately, issues-based questions support the leader's core sales philosophy, which holds that sales, for the most part, has a lot less to do with products and services than it has to do with relationships that are focused on areas of mutual opportunity. When you ask these kinds of questions, you're showing that you are committed, not "to closing the sale," but to learning all that you need to know about this person's critical goals and plans. You're not acquiring this information merely to earn a commission or get a new client (although those are nice byproducts), but also so that you can build up a relationship that's based on securing long-term benefits for both parties involved.

The ability to look beyond short-term outcomes is one of the key traits of effective leaders. It's the reason people sign on to the idea of having a business relationship with you. So why on Earth would you want to begin the relationship with short-term, status-based questions? Who gets inspired by those?

The Leader's Wisdom

Leadership is based on a spiritual quality; the power to inspire others to follow.—Vince Lombardi

---

Issues-Based Questions Affect Everything

Several years ago, I held a seminar where one of the participants was a senior manager for a top national jewelry chain. He challenged me to come up with an issues-based question that would improve his ability to connect with retail customers.

I've had some experience in this area. There were times when I wanted to buy my wife some jewelry as a gift, but was unsure about what kind would fit the moment. The salesperson would typically ask me what type of jewelry I was looking for. Wrong question! I didn't know that yet. By asking me a question like this, the salesperson was focused more on the merchandise than on me. What he really wanted to ask about was the *message* I wanted to send to my wife.

So here's what I said to the manager at that seminar: "Suppose that, instead of saying 'Can I help you?'—which is the way your salespeople are currently opening the conversation—they found a way to ask a question that honed in on what the other person was trying to say by buying jewelry?"

At this point, we did a little role-play. I acted as the clerk, and the manager played the customer. It sounded something like this:

Clerk: Welcome to Smith's! May I ask who the special person is that you have in mind today?

Customer: Yes, my wife.

Clerk: Oh, that's wonderful. Please, tell me about the occasion and the message you want to communicate with this piece of jewelry.

Customer: Well, let me think about that. I don't know ... maybe I want to show her that I love her, because you can never say that too often. Every time she looks at this piece, I definitely want her to know that I love her. But I also want to say that in a way that's unique and that celebrates all the time we've had together. I want to give her something I haven't given her before.

(Now that the clerk understands the outcome and the message that this customer is trying to communicate with his purchase. She can easily move to a status-based question.)

Clerk: That's great. How long have you been married?

Customer: It will be 18 years next August.

Clerk: Congratulations! That's really great. Can I ask what you've given her in the past?

Customer: Earrings, rings. That's pretty much it.

Clerk: So you don't want to do that again.

Customer: No.

Clerk: Okay. Have you thought about a watch? After all, watches are the one thing most of us look at all the time during the course of the day. Your "I love you" message will come through loud and clear, again and again, each and every day. And, of course, you'd be saying something important about the time you've spent together as man and wife. Would you like to take a look at our watches?

Customer: Sure, that's a good idea. Let's start there.

Who is the leader in this conversation? The salesperson! And how did the salesperson establish leadership? Not by spending 20 minutes trying to break the ice, and not by talking about random pieces of jewelry that added nothing to the customer's value perception. She immediately asked questions that would allow her to discover what the customer wanted to accomplish with this particular product. Notice that the issues-based question drove the rest of the conversation. Notice, too, how quickly the information was uncovered. Here, once again, is the question that made that great discussion possible. Look at it closely: "Please, tell me about the *occasion* and the *message* you want to communicate with this piece of jewelry."

By gathering this information up front, the clerk guided the customer in several ways: by helping him to figure out what he wanted in the first place, and then by offering products that would meet his needs.

The Magic of "Three"

A particularly powerful issues-based question revolves around the idea of asking the prospect to "identify three things" from a particular area or within a specific category.

Look once again at the financial services example I shared with you a little earlier in the chapter and you'll see that I crafted such a question for this group. It sounded like this: "What are the three things you want your money to provide for you in the future?" Whenever sales professionals ask a question that gives them only one possible answer, they will usually find they have little to talk about. On the other hand, if the answer uncovers three issues, there is more room to uncover an area where they can add value.

Years of experience have taught me that there is special power in building an issues-based question around the number three. Psychologically, people respond well to the numbers 3, 5, and 7. That's why speakers often discuss "the three points we will cover today . . ." As for the issues-based question, I have personally found the number three to be the lucky charm. Asking people to come up with three variations on their response almost always adds energy and direction to the conversation.

Transform the Conversation

Issues-based questions have a way of turning things around immediately. I once did a one-hour talk for a group of financial veteran advisors. After the program, one advisor called two prospects from his hotel room, each of whom was a widow who had about $100,000 to invest. Neither of these women had secured anyone's services yet as a financial advisor. This was a major decision, and they were making it without the aid of a loved one who had recently passed away. Establishing trust and eliminating risk were still big issues. The widows were interested in hearing more, but they were not yet comfortable enough to give the financial advisor their business.

This advisor had one of these ladies on his radar screen for three months and the other for six months. His message to them that night was simple. He explained that although he had spent most of his time with them up to this point talking about stocks and bonds, he realized that he had really failed to ask them the most important question of all—the question that had prompted him to arrange the conference call. When they asked him what that question was, he said, "What are the three things you want your money to provide for you in the future?"

The floodgates opened! Instantly, the women began sharing all kinds of critical information with him about their financial goals. They offered information that he never uncovered before. He started building a level of trust he didn't have with them at this point. All of a sudden, both of those prospects felt comfortable enough to commit their funds to him *on the phone, that night*. Now, that is true sales leadership!

"Do You Mean I Can *Never* Ask Status-Based Questions?"

When salespeople hear my passionate endorsement of issues-based questions as the best kinds of inquiries with which to open the sales discussion, they sometimes think I believe that status-based questions are always off limits. Not so! As I've said, status-based questions definitely have their place, as do three other kinds of questions: illustrative questions, clarification questions, and consequence questions. However, *all* of these must be preceded by a powerful issues-based question.

> ### The Leader's Advantage
>
> Issues-based questions are all about where we want to go, while status based questions are all about where we currently are.

Take a look at the diagram in Figure 7.2.

Notice that we start with the issues-based question. We can then pose a status-based question as necessary. Remember: Starting with the issues-based question will enhance your overall value.

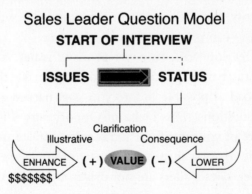

Figure 7.2

Delta of Opportunity

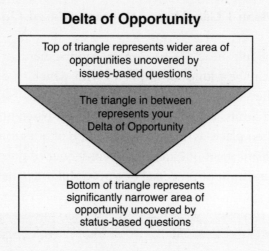

Figure 7.3

The Delta of Opportunity

Sales leaders use questions to expand what I call the *Delta of Opportunity*. The Merriam Webster Dictionary defines "delta" as "something shaped like a triangle." The zone of opportunity we're discussing is also shaped like a triangle. In this questioning model, the more issues you can identify, the greater the opportunity you will have to find areas where you can provide valuable solutions.

This is why you want to cover as many issues as possible *before* you ask a status-based question; so you can make the top of that triangle as broad as possible before you start narrowing it by asking status-based questions! This Delta of Opportunity will allow you to cross-sell more of your products and services, create more value, and achieve a wider market share with your customer (see Figure 7.3).

Remember, sales leaders are not driven by transactions. They are compelled to maximize the impact on their customer's lives. And when they do that, they generate greater market share for themselves and their organizations.

Let's look more closely at the kinds of questions you can use to expand your Delta of Opportunity.

Illustrative Questions

These questions encourage the prospect or customer to "paint a picture" or fill in the blanks. They give us a better sense of the other person's point of view. Illustrative questions help you fill in the picture of how your prospect sees the world, and they help you ensure that your picture is the same as theirs. You want to add as much depth to that image as possible. The more details you know about the prospect's view, the better you can respond.

A few years ago, I went to see the Tony-Award winning musical *The Will Rogers Follies*. During the show, the actor playing Will Rogers shared what I thought was an important selling lesson. He mentioned the habit of Native Americans who were willing to go an extra step in expressing themselves to another person. Instead of simply hearing their counterpart and responding in kind, they would hear the initial response and then walk right behind that person to get a view of exactly what that person was looking at. Only then—once they had literally seen the world from the other person's perspective—would they respond.

If this story isn't actually true, it should be. How many salespeople take the time to truly look at things from the prospect's point of view? How clear is your view of your customer's world? If you are missing bits of information that will take away from the clarity and depth of your customer's view, you will not be in a position to enlarge your Delta of Opportunity.

Illustrative questions also allow you to soften your questioning approach. By asking someone to share or describe for you their view of the world, the exchange becomes more of a casual conversation and less of a series of hard-core questions.

The word "share" is particularly powerful when you're formulating these kinds of questions: "Can you share your thoughts with me about what's working best in your procurement process right now?" People love to share feelings, experiences, and stories. They are much more reluctant to divulge information. Remember, part of a sales leader's job is to create a comfortable and inviting environment—an environment in which people *want* to share information and feel safe in doing so.

Other examples of illustrative questions might be:

"Can you please describe what this project would look like if everything went perfectly?"

"Can you share some thoughts on how you plan to measure the success of this project?"

"Please share with me what a typical day would look like in your ideal retirement scenario."

The Clarification Question

This is very similar to the illustrative question. The difference is that this time you're asking the prospect for his or her *definition* of a specific word or term.

A few years ago, my wife, daughter, and I were on our way to vacation in Cape Cod and decided to stop on the road for something to eat. We saw a sign for this great Scottish restaurant you may have heard of before: McDonalds. Upon entering, my wife took my daughter to sit down, but first gave me her order. A Quarter Pounder, fries and a Diet Coke. As she walked away, she reminded me several times to get her "a lot of ketchup."

To me, "a lot of ketchup" meant many of those little packets. When I brought the food to the table, my wife looked at me with a grin and proclaimed that I gotten her the wrong kind of ketchup. Puzzled, I asked her what the right kind of ketchup might look like. Without batting an eye, she said, "The kind that comes in a cup!"

Based on the way that I was looking at the world when she asked for "a lot of ketchup," I wasn't even considering walking over to the counter that had hundreds of little cups stacked next to a ketchup dispenser with a push handle. That was, however, exactly what my wife had in mind. Why was this important for my wife? She didn't want the hassle of opening those pesky little packets, which would probably squirt ketchup all over her clothes. She also wanted to dip her French fries *into* the ketchup, and she wanted to take as much as she wanted. But instead of a convenient cup, she got dozens of little packets, and she was disappointed with the outcome. I had made a classic selling mistake by giving my wife what I "knew" she needed (the ketchup), but not giving it to her in the way she wanted it! In selling terms, I had offered the wrong solution. As a result, I had not met her expectations.

This has happened to me in a business setting, and I'm sure it's happened to you, too. The client wants one thing; we serve up something different, something that's based on the way we're looking at the situation. Why? Because we're too lazy to ask someone to clarify what she means when she uses a common phrase that we think we understand—for instance, "a lot of ketchup."

Face it: You are going to hear the same words over and over again in your daily routine. Prospects and customers are going to ask you for speed of delivery, quality, safety, the best price, and a dozen other things that you're going to think you understand. Even though these people are going to be using the same words, however, each one of them will be associating different meanings to those words. You have to clarify exactly what each and every person really means.

One day a few years ago I received calls from two prospects inquiring about my services as a motivational speaker. The calls came within 90 minutes of each other and used exactly the same words: motivational speech. I asked each prospect to share with me exactly what they wanted to accomplish by having a motivational speaker fly out to talk to their sales team. What were the outcomes they wanted the "motivational speech" to deliver?

I got two very different answers. One prospect explained that it had been a tough year at his company, but they'd finally turned the corner. At their annual meeting, they just wanted their sales team to laugh, relax, and let go of the stress. They wanted heavy entertainment—and not a lot of content. That's what they meant when they said "motivational speech."

The other company said almost exactly the opposite. They, too, had had a tough year, but instead of entertainment, they wanted me to share a lot of good ideas, tactics, and strategies that their salespeople could assimilate—and then use—in order to turn their company's fortunes around. That's what they wanted from a motivational speaker—someone who would pass along the right tools for the salespeople's toolbox and then motivate them to use those tools.

This same phrase ended up having two entirely different meanings for each of these audiences. Imagine what might have happened if I hadn't clarified what each caller meant! My approach with each prospect had to be different, and yours does, too. Ask questions like:

- "You just said that 'quality' was very important to you. What, exactly does 'quality' mean to you?"

Follow Will Rogers' advice: Clarify what your prospects and customers are saying, so you can see the world from their point of view and get a sharper image of what your prospect or customer is looking at. The more precise the image, the bigger your Delta of Opportunity will be.

The Consequence Question

I'll be sharing everything you need to know about this extremely important principle of establishing consequences—or outcomes—later on, when we talk about the value proposition. For now, all you have to remember is that consequence questions are questions that introduce positive change.

Sales leaders rely on these kinds of questions almost as heavily as they do on issues-based questions. The big difference is that consequence questions tend to come when the leader wants to shine a spotlight on the real-world consequences the customer would face by choosing not to work with the leader.

While this may sound ominous, it really isn't. Every action creates a reaction; every decision carries a consequence. Assessing and prioritizing the inevitable consequences of a decision is one of the places where the sales leader adds value.

Obviously, timing is crucial for these kinds of questions and so is the context in which you ask them. The more reality-based and compelling the consequences you establish for the prospects are, the more powerful and compelling your case will be.

To understand how the sales leader uses consequence questions, you really have to understand the larger concept of the value proposition. That's why I'm going to save my examples of what these kinds of questions look like for the next chapter.

No Scripts!

The Leader's Advantage

Sales leaders do not use scripts. Instead, they work an agenda.

Scripts are inherently self-focused. People who use them are only worried about saying what they have to say and are rarely listening attentively to the other person.

An agenda is something very different. It allows you to position yourself as the sales leader, identify the goals of your customers, determine your Delta of Opportunity, and begin working your way toward valuable solutions. Whether you ask a clarification, illustrative, or a consequence question as a supporting query will depend on the answers that your customers are giving you. If your next question does not support the answer you just received, then you're not using your agenda intelligently! All you are doing is sending a signal to your prospect that you are not listening. That's when the prospect will mentally shut down on you.

The Leader's Advantage

Don't enter the sales interview with preconceived notions about the questions you must ask or attempt to predict the answers you will receive. Be open and flexible. Be present for your customer!

Listen to the Answers

Unfortunately, most salespeople don't really *listen* to the answers their prospects give them. They only *hear* the answers, and there's a difference.

Hearing is taking what somebody says and relating it to what you already know or what you think the person is saying. When you simply hear an answer, you attach your assumptions to what you believe the answer means. You will confirm (agree with the message) or discount (disagree with the message) based solely on your own interpretation. You will not take into account the intent of the person who is speaking.

Listening takes hearing to a whole new level. When you are listening, there are no assumptions. You clear your mind of all thoughts, biases, and opinions and open yourself to your customer's unique intention and point of view—neither of which you could possibly know about ahead of time. As a result, you gain an accurate picture of your customer's world by leaving yourself open to explore the nuances, biases, and opinions your customers are attaching to the words they use.

Hearing is reactive. Listening is proactive.

Let me give you an example that will illustrate the difference. As you know, my last name is Karr. Whenever I check in for a flight, check into a hotel, pick up a rental car, or show up at a restaurant to claim a reservation I've made, I always do two things. First, I say my name, right out loud, "Karr," and then I spell it, "K-A-R-R."

Nine times out of 10, the person I am talking to will inform me that I have no reservation. At that point, I ask, "Did you look under C or K?" Then I'll spell my name again. I'll say, "It's Karr— K-A-R-R." At that point, the person invariably admits to looking under the letter "C" not the letter "K," which is how I just told them—a few seconds ago—to spell my name!

It's astonishing to me how often this happens. There I am, spelling it out for them, yet time after time, they will only hear my name based on how they think it should be spelled. There is no listening taking place.

You spell the customer's name wrong at your own risk. What you think and how you would do things is irrelevant. Take the time to listen—not just hear—what your customer is trying to say to you.

There are people like my colleague, Lyman Steil PhD, who have built a successful career around the subject of listening. Needless to say, the few paragraphs I have passed along here do not do full justice to the topic. Even so, I hope you get the message that listening must be a core behavior that weaves its way throughout the fabric of a sales call. You simply cannot be an effective sales leader if you don't make a conscious effort to listen to what others are telling you.

What's the Intent?

Discovering your potential client's true intent can make the difference between closing the deal and losing it. Discovering the true intent can determine whether you will deliver the right solution and hold on to a customer for life or convey the wrong solution and lose the customer forever.

A vice president of sales for a major supplier of heavy equipment called me in to assist with a difficult negotiation. They were looking to renew a $5 million contract with a railroad. The railroad was losing money, and its board of directors had issued an edict that all contracts would be cut by 18 percent. They figured the totality of the savings would push them into the black. My client, unfortunately, was in no position to reduce prices and had to at least stay even. My client also had technology that could put four times the proposed cost savings back into the railroad's bottom line.

At this point, the customer didn't want to hear about any of that. They had hired a professional negotiator whose job was clear: get this 18 percent price concession from all vendors, including my client—no ifs, ands, or buts.

I asked the client to tell me what he thought the real issue was. His answer: the 18 percent price cut. I disagreed; I didn't think that was the real issue. The real issue, I argued, was that the railroad needed to get back into the black.

The across-the-board price cuts were the railroad's solution to the big issue; that was how the railroad had decided to get where it wanted to go. My client had heard the customer ask for the 18 percent price cut all right, but he had not listened to the customer's intent. As a result, he was now negotiating on the wrong issue—an issue he could not concede. There was nowhere for the conversation to go but downhill!

I suggested to the client that he go into the next meeting and ask this question: "What is the most important thing that we could do for you? Give you an 18 percent price cut, which will yield a certain amount of savings, or provide you with a solution guaranteed to add four times that amount to your bottom line?" After he had posed that question, I instructed my client to stop talking.

What do you think the answer was? All of a sudden, the railroad wanted to hear more about the technology that would add that amount to their bottom line. This question allowed the client to move off the issue of the price cut and into a conversation about the underlying intent: getting the railroad back in the black.

What's interesting about this scenario is that my client had been telling the customer all about this technology for months, but the customer was simply not in a frame of mind to listen. The hired gun was under pressure to produce those 18 percent price cuts. My client hadn't figured out a way to get him to look at the issue differently until he posed this question, which prompted the client to motivate his customer to look at the bigger picture. The hired gun now saw an opportunity to generate even more savings and become a hero. This issues-based question transformed the conversation, changed the landscape, and ultimately produced a contract extension.

Do you ever find yourself trying to negotiate issues you cannot resolve? Do your conversations with a certain prospect ever seem to go nowhere? If so, maybe it is time for you to listen more closely to your customer's or prospect's intent. Remember, it is not the words people use that count. It is the intent that drives their decisions.

Sales Leaders Never Stop Asking Issues-Based Questions

Salespeople have a regrettable tendency to cease focusing on their customer's needs once they get their business. They forget to take the actions that won them the business in the first place. They stop listening, stop asking the right questions, and stop analyzing their customer's intent. Before they know it their business is deteriorating and the competition is coming in through the back door.

As a leader, you must remain focused on your customer's current issues, no matter how long you've been working with that particular customer. You must keep in mind that your clients are not interested in what you have done for them in the past; they want to know what you are going to do for them *today* and in the future. This may sound like a cliché, but it's nevertheless something that veteran salespeople routinely ignore!

Every time you meet with a customer, you must ask the issues-based questions that will identify the new challenges facing your customers are confronting. You must help them illustrate their new goals, clarify their positions, and determine the consequences of not dealing effectively. Remember, the moment the customer starts to feel the benefits of switching vendors outweigh the penalties or inconveniences of canceling your agreement, you are history!

The Leader's Advantage

Leaders ask questions that treat customers like prospects. They never take customers for granted, and they continuously look for the new Delta of Opportunity that will provide new solutions and enhance existing solutions.

Your Chapter Seven Commitment

Since this is a chapter on questions, I want you to answer the following questions on your Commitment Sheet.

1. What outcomes are you looking to achieve by asking better questions?
2. What three issues-based questions are you committed to asking on your sales calls today and in the future?
3. What new commitments are you willing to make and keep in order to best serve your clients, based on the information provided in this chapter?

COMMITMENT!

(Pronunciation: ko-'mit-mint, Function: noun, Definition: a: an agreement or pledge to do something in the future; b: something pledged c: the state or an instance of being obligated or emotionally impelled, a commitment to a cause)

_____

_____

_____

_____

_____

_____

_____

_____

_____

_____

_____

_____

_____

_____

_____

_____

_____

_____

_____

For more of these sample sheets go to http://www.leadsellorgetoutoftheway.com.

Figure 7.4 Commitment Sheet

8 | Creating Powerful Value Propositions

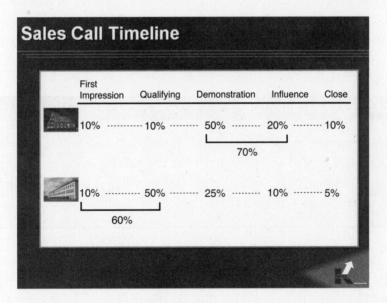

Figure 8.1

You are still in the qualifying stage! You are still not yet ready to make any kind of recommendation. By postponing the transition into demonstration (which takes place when you present your products and services), you are actually reducing the overall length of your sales cycle. The sales cycle, of course, is the period that elapses between the time when you first uncover the opportunity and the time when you close a deal. Reducing this cycle will allow you to sell more in less time at higher profit. The sooner you close the deal, the less time, resources, and effort you will have to spend on that deal . . . and the sooner you can move on to another one.

In this chapter, you will learn about the value propositions you create for prospects and customers. If you do not establish your value proposition before you move on to demonstration, then your sales cycle will drag on and on. You will not be using the leader's sales model, but rather the follower's sales model.

All too often, salespeople and other influencers try to move much too quickly into the demonstration phase, before they have created a powerful value proposition or any value proposition at all. The result: They kill the opportunity.

The Leader's Advantage

A "powerful value proposition" is simply a compelling reason that will propel the customer over the barrier of complacency and onto the path of change. This decision is driven by a belief that working with you can create better results.

Most salespeople, as I say, make the mistake of presenting before they have articulated—or even thought about—this value proposition. I've come to believe that they do this for two main reasons: first, to satisfy their own need to talk, a need that is typically driven by stress or the mistaken belief that they are "in control" of the exchange when they are talking; and second, the difficult predicament in which their own companies put them. Organizations spend lots of money, time, and energy training their salespeople on all the specifications, features, and benefits of the products and services they sell. Salespeople are, of course, expected to communicate all that information to prospects. However, what everyone up and down the organization needs to understand is that before any of this information can become relevant to the sales conversation, the salesperson *must* find out what's most important to the prospect and why! Great features, benefits, and specs may end up being critical. But in a sales call, they are secondary to the customer's perceived opinion of what is necessary, wanted, and desired. That means that salespeople must wait until we have asked the prospect the right questions and developed a compelling reason for change (value proposition) based on those questions to begin demonstrating to our prospects why our products will solve their problems.

What's Still Missing?

The key to creating a powerful value proposition lies in the unique information that we uncover about a specific prospect. Before we launch any kind of presentation or recommendation, we have to ask ourselves what critical information is still missing about this person's world. If we used the question categories in the previous chapter, we now know (in very broad terms) where the customer wants to go and what she is trying to achieve. We got her to paint a clear and concise picture of what success would look like. We clarified the meanings of the words she used to describe her desired outcomes. But we don't yet have everything; there's still an important component missing, namely her perception of the *impacts* that will result from her decision. Until we know that, we cannot create our value proposition, and we cannot make any kind of recommendation.

This is one of the most important concepts you will ever master as a professional salesperson. Most salespeople can't wait to talk about what they can do for their customers. They are eager to discuss their products, features, solutions, and they want desperately to share the past successes that are just like this situation. But as sales leaders, we must wait to talk about those things and postpone that conversation until we have gotten a sense of the prospect's assessment of all the implications—positive and negative—that connect to the buying decision.

If you short-circuit the process by trying to skip over the part where you figure out what the prospect thinks will happen if he or she doesn't make the right call, then your solution will land with little or no impact in the prospect's world.

> ### The Leader's Advantage
>
> The question is not whether or not your solution is sound. The question is whether your solution lands with impact in this prospect's world.

Believe me when I tell you that your ideas will only have an effect if the customer is verbally, mentally, and physically engaged in the conversation in a way that provides you with the information you need from this person concerning the potential impact of a wrong decision. Years ago, I was negotiating the sale of a condominium in which I had lived. After asking a few questions of the realtor, I found out the bidder had just sold his house and needed to close quickly. I also found out that, being the only unit available with a view of Manhattan, the bidder really wanted my condo. Armed with this information, I did not back down on my price when the bidder came in with a low offer. I simply asked the realtor how he would feel if he let this opportunity slip through his fingers. What did I know about the realtor's situation that enabled me to ask that question? Well, I knew that if the realtor and bidder walked away, they would be losing out on the opportunity to get the bidder into what they both knew was the right condo—in a hurry!

(You could make the case that, if she'd been a better negotiator, the realtor would never have shared such sensitive information with me up front, but that's a different discussion.) I never would have uncovered that information if I hadn't asked the right questions from the outset.

This may seem like an aggressive example, but I think you can see why it's an appropriate one. Your value proposition must be rooted not just in any generic solution, but in terms of the specific issues that the prospect has discussed with you. It must go beyond addressing generic concerns of the typical customer to whom you sell and speak to the particular interests of the person you've been talking to. If you build a custom-fitted value proposition in this way, how can the prospect possibly refute what you are saying or brush you off without examining your ideas in depth? You are directly addressing issues and concerns the prospect has verbalized first, and, as a result, you have likely won his undivided attention. That attention is a critical factor for your success because it makes it much more likely that the prospect will emerge as an active collaborator in crafting the solution you eventually implement together.

Which scenario do you think will lead to a higher closing ratio: one in which you are pushing your thoughts and ideas onto the customer without developing any meaningful case, or justification, in support of your solution? Or one in which the customer *helps* you create the case, and thereby invites you to share ideas on how to solve her problems? Obviously, the second option is preferable. With that point firmly in mind, do what I tell my audiences to do whenever they feel the urge to talk too much and too soon: Sit on your hands and shut up!

From this point forward in the chapter, my job is to show you how to create a unique value proposition that connects to information you've developed with a specific prospect. If you're interested in learning how to do this—and by this point I certainly hope that you are—then you are going to have to buy in, without reservation, to a concept that throws some salespeople: the concept of the consequence of choices.

The Consequence of the Prospect's Choices

Focusing patiently but firmly on the consequence of the prospect's choices helps you point the way toward the right consequence question, and allows you to create a unique, compelling value proposition that fits your prospect like a glove.

The value proposition that you create for a customer is simply an illustration that highlights the value of working with you as compared to the results of not working with you. It should cast a clear light on the consequences of the prospect's choice to go down one path rather than another. While some people feel that the word "consequence" has a negative connotation—and often link it with the idea of bashing the competition, pressuring the prospect, or other manipulative, high-pressure selling tactics—that kind of selling is not what I'm talking about here!

Webster's Dictionary defines the word "consequence" as "something produced by a cause or necessarily following from a set of conditions." That's really all we're looking at here: cause and effect, gain and loss, choice and consequence—all of which are based on the information we get from this particular prospect. Leaders know that every choice carries a consequence and pose their questions accordingly.

The Consequence Question

So what is the consequence question? Essentially, it's the result of all of your prior work. It's very important to you as a leader, because it's focused powerfully on change, which is a topic near and dear to the heart of every effective leader, no matter what his or her field or industry focus may be. In the final analysis, all leaders are really salespeople, and what they are selling is change, with "change" being defined as a better result, not simply change for its own sake. If we are truly effective leaders, then we sell constructive change by means of consequence questions and work our way toward a clear value proposition that dramatically justifies the kind of change we have in mind.

You Are Asking People to Change!

Although you may not realize it, whenever you ask someone who has never worked with you before to put aside all the other things he's doing and reserve a slot in his calendar to hear what you have to say, you're asking that person to change.

Whenever you ask people to alter the way they're doing something—pay more money than they're used to paying, work with people they haven't yet worked with, learn systems they have not yet mastered—you are asking them to change.

Whenever you challenge someone to think of you as a resource for something you haven't provided before, you're asking that person to change.

In each and every case, you must be honest with yourself. From the prospect's point of view, how persuasive is the justification you are offering for the change you want to make?

Most salespeople seriously underestimate the difficulty of the change they are asking the prospect to make and seriously overestimate the persuasive power of the reasons for change that they have offered (or, more likely, simply assumed).

Change Can Be Painful!

This is a critical point. Selling, by nature, involves change, and change, by nature, is painful. How painful does the customer perceive the change to be? And what is that pain going to be compared to?

Read it again: For the buyer, there is always going to be pain associated with, for instance, learning to use new products and services. There is always going to be a feeling of uneasiness in not knowing exactly what will happen next; although prospects hear the promises, they have yet to see the results. They will undoubtedly experience some discomfort with the political risk of standing behind a new vendor. After all, even if your prospects aren't 100 percent satisfied with their present vendor, they at least know what to expect. They may think that they're "better off with the devil we know than the devil we don't know." And last but certainly not least, there is always the prospect of experiencing pain when prices are increased.

So why on Earth is the buyer going to sign on to experience any of that pain? There has to be a good reason! People usually don't consciously volunteer to experience pain for its own sake. Leaders know they have to come up with a convincing answer to the question, "Why should I put myself through this?"

That's where the consequence question comes in and gets the prospect to focus clearly on the question of which outcome will be more uncomfortable for her in the end: staying where she is and not realizing the results you have to offer or going through the pain of change and reaping the benefits of working with you!

When the consequences (i.e., the results) of inaction are seen as too high a price to pay, people will take action to change their situation. On the other hand, when inaction is seen as being less painful than the pain of taking action, people will not take action to change.

What Is the Consequence of Not Working with You?

A consequence question focuses compellingly, and without any apology whatsoever, on the cost of not working with you. Each consequence question you ask must be targeted closely to an individual prospect. You cannot expect to develop a single consequence question that will work for all of your customers. (By the way, if you turned to this section of the book in the hope of finding the one "magic bullet" question that would transform any selling situation, I'm sorry to disappoint you. That question does not exist!)

A consequence question builds on a line of discussion that has already established the need for change in the prospect's world, and that is required for the customer to achieve different results.

The perceived discomfort associated with the salesperson's proposed change is not limited to costs alone. However, because I want to give you a simple example, let me start by sharing the development of a consequence question that revolves around cost.

It might evolve like this:

"Mr. Prospect, you mentioned that part of the reason you're talking to me today is that you are eager to avoid the financial costs that would connect to a catastrophic data loss. Specifically, how high would that financial cost be to your organization, in terms of a worst-case scenario?" (Notice that we are asking the customer to clarify what his perception of the cost would be).

Now, suppose this is the answer: "I'd say the potential downside from a total system collapse would be at least $300 million."

Can you see where you should be going with this next? That $300 million figure is very, very important. It's going to be the centerpiece of your value proposition because it's the consequence question that expresses that value proposition in quantifiable terms that are specific to the client. Let's say that the investment in your project is $10 million. That seems like a lot of money until you compare it to the $300 million the company is going to have to pay to recover from a catastrophic data loss.

Therefore, when push comes to shove, you're going to ask the prospect a consequence question that sounds something like this:

"Are you really willing to give up $300 million dollars in potential productivity losses to avoid an investment of $10 million?"

Now, because sales leadership is an art and not a science, you don't have to say exactly those words to the prospect. Sales leadership is about making the case for change, and doing so in whatever terms you feel comfortable with. However, you will want to point your individually tailored consequence question in the same direct direction as the question you just read. You could, of course, decide to frame the issue differently, based on your own personal style and the rapport you've built up with the prospect. Consider this alternative: "Getting $300 million for a $10 million investment would be considered by many as being a tremendous return on investment, wouldn't you say?"

When the prospect verbalizes the potential consequence of $300 million by not accepting your solution, he has volunteered and confirmed the harsh realities of his world. You must build a value proposition—and a corresponding consequence question—around those realities, and you must address his unique situation in light of how much more pleasant you and your product can make that reality.

Build Up to the Consequence Question

Of course, you can't begin the sales discussion with that consequence question. You must lead the prospect along until it is a natural landing point of the conversation. If you begin the conversation by presenting the product first and the price second, and then try to use the consequence question as a closing tool, you will find yourself back out on the street in a hurry. On the other hand, if you get the customer comfortable talking to you about where he is trying to go—and stating in his own words exactly what's at risk if he doesn't get there—then you will probably find your prospect responding more favorably to your eventual consequence question.

You should start working toward the question as soon as you know that the prospect has (a) given you, in his own words, the information you need to formulate it; and (b) prepared himself psychologically to hear a frank discussion of both the upsides and downsides of the situation.

If you ask subtle consequence questions along the way that help the prospect to look more deeply and honestly at both sides of the equation he or she is facing, you won't sound as though you're trying to box the person into a corner. The ideal situation is for both you and the prospect to look at the situation and to work together collaboratively to identify the best path forward.

Again, it is absolutely crucial that the *prospect* verbalize what's at stake if he or she does not take action.

The Value Equation

Take another look at the equation we discussed earlier in this book:

$$CNC - CC = PV$$

The cost of no change minus the cost of change equals perceived value.

This is the value equation, and it's a blueprint for your value proposition.

As a leader, you will use consequence questions to highlight the specific results that an individual prospect will face by not taking action on a particular recommendation you make. That's the cost of no change. Then subtract from that the cost of change, which will be the better result your customer will achieve from working with you.

The difference between the cost of what you offer and the cost of not taking action equates to the perceived value of your solution, and the more realistic and compelling this perceived value is (i.e., the more closely it is connected to the prospect's world) then the more powerful your value equation will be, and the easier it will be for the prospect to conclude, on his or her own, that the cost of inaction is simply too high

The Leader's Advantage

Remember, consequence questions can't stand alone, and they certainly can't be the only questions you ask a prospect or customer. You must set them up properly using the questions we discussed in Chapter 6.

Don't Try to Use a Script to Set Up Your Consequence Question!

The leader's sales interview process should always remain fluid. As I've mentioned earlier, it's an intuitive process, not one that's script driven. Leaders are spontaneous and interactive during the sales interview; they are never the prisoners of a predetermined checklist of questions.

That said, let's look at the general sequence that a sales call might follow. You will ask an issues-based question at some early point in the conversation. Whether you ask a clarification question, an illustrative

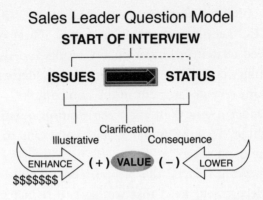

Figure 8.2

question, or a consequence question depends on the situation you're facing, the concerns the other person has raised, and your ongoing sense of the way the sales interview is unfolding. See the very general summary of what the questioning sequence might look like in Figure 8.2.

Now let's look at that graphic closely. It's worth studying as long as we remember that we must never enter the interview with any preconceived notion about what order the prospect or customer is supposed to follow. However, we can look at how the leader's sales interview process might play out, and one way is like this.

1. Having established some rapport, the leader asks at least one issues-based question.
2. In response to those questions, the prospect opens up and feels comfortable sharing information about his or her situation.
3. At some point, the prospect says something about a specific goal that's important to him or her: "We want to increase the

quality of our customer experience, but we also want to help our CEO keep our shareholders happy. That's our challenge. We need to deliver higher quality results and also reduce our operating costs. That goes for me in my department, and it goes for every department in the company."

4. The leader might then ask a clarification question: "Tell me something, by how much would you want to reduce your operating expenses?"

5. At this point, maybe the prospect says, "The CEO has told each department head that we have to reduce our operating costs by at least 20 percent. In my department, that equates to about $2 million this year."

6. A good consequence question in response to this might sound like the following: "So what would you say the impacts would be if you weren't able to reach your 20 percent cost-cutting goal this year?"

7. The prospect might respond, "Well, the CEO has been pretty clear about that. If we don't hit the cost-cutting target, he's going to have no other alternative than to start restructuring the workforce."

8. The leader might then pose a clarification question: "What would 'restructuring the workforce' mean specifically in your department?"

9. The prospect might answer: "If we miss our goal by 5 percent—in other words, if we post only a 15 percent reduction in expenses, which would actually be a bit of a stretch to do—the CEO has told me personally that I'm going to have to let approximately 20 people go."

10. The leader might continue with a consequence question: "Let me ask you something else. How would working with 20 fewer employees affect your obligation to deliver the same level of satisfaction to your customers?"

Obviously, the consequence questions set the stage for the value proposition, the compelling reason for the customer doing something different than what they're currently doing. I've shared this much of the sample dialogue with you so that you can see the direction the leader's questions are always headed. At the end of the day, remembering the direction is more important than remembering the names of the categories of questions the leader asks. Can you see how it works? The idea is to uncover as many consequences of inaction as possible, so that the customer perceives the cost of not accepting your proposal as far greater than the investment in your solution.

Let's say that you and the prospect have agreed that the software, hardware, and training package that your company provides have the perfect track record and the right customization options for this company. You both know it's the right solution; it will allow the company to both hit the CEO's goal of reducing operating expenditures by 20 percent and actually improve customer satisfaction. Those are the results that are at stake if the prospect doesn't buy your product.

The moment everyone knew was coming finally rolls around. The prospect says, "Okay, how much is this going to run me?"

1. Your answer: "The value for that system, including the training, customization, and follow-through sessions, is going to be $330,000."
2. The prospect is taken aback. "That seems kind of expensive. As you know, we're under some cash constraints here."
3. You ask, "What did you think the investment was going to be?"
4. The prospect says, "Well, I was shooting for something closer to $250,000."

5. You say, "Let me ask you this: Are you really willing to sacrifice a solution that we've established will get you to the $2 million in operating cost reductions that your CEO is looking for, improve your customer's experience, and keep you from having to lay off 20 people all because of an $80,000 difference in price?" Again, whether or not you use these words and this tone is up to you, but you must raise these points somehow. Your job is simply to communicate your message in as positive and compelling a manner as possible.

Now, let's suppose you do this and the prospect says, "I need your solution, but my budget is only $X." You should then ask the customer, "What are you willing to give up in the solution we're looking at?"

Usually, the prospect will say, "Give up? I can't give up anything. I need the whole thing."

This is the point at which you must protect your value. You must say something like, "If you are not willing to give up anything and you need the solution as is, then you will be making an investment of $Y." (That's your original price.) You can continue: "If you want to give some things up, maybe we can then lower your cost. But remember, you will be taking away things that were inserted to help you reach your overall goal."

Welcome to Leadership Negotiating 101! When prospects are asked what they would be willing to give up for a lower price, they often say, "Nothing," and will often end up buying the whole package for the original price. (That's assuming the salesperson did not discount the product or service already.) In the event there really is a budget constraint, you are offering your customer a means for getting some help in dealing with his issues. But you are not giving your service away for nothing.

> **The Leader's Advantage**
>
> Never negotiate against yourself. If you have to discount, always get something in return. You and you alone have the power and the responsibility to protect your value.

Do You Fear the Consequence Question?

Some salespeople shy away from asking or even thinking about consequence questions because they consider them to be too confrontational. Here's my question: If there is no consequence, no downside to the status quo—if the results the prospect faces in working with you are not positive—then why should you ask the person to change what they're doing? After all, why would anyone make any kind of change if there was not a clear advantage to doing so?

For example: Would you choose to get a different kind of car if you hadn't identified a better result you wanted from your driving experience—something that your current car did not provide for you? Even if you're leasing, not buying, and your lease is up, when it's time to make a decision about your car, are you going to lease exactly the same kind of car again or are you going to change somehow? Let's say you decide to downgrade, because you want to enhance your financial well-being. That's you pursuing a better result and avoiding one you don't like. It's like this with every choice in your life. Would you change the phone service you use if there were no better results waiting for you on the other side of your decision to change? Would you change the store where you buy your groceries if you couldn't identify a better result that connected to making that change?

Leaders are all about inspiring change, which inevitably means looking closely at the difference between what's happening now and what better outcome could result if change occurred. Leaders understand that when it comes to motivating human beings, people are not moved to take action unless they want to remove pain or gain pleasure. If it helps you to think of consequence questions as spotlighting the pleasure people are finally going to get to when they stop feeling the pain, I have no problem with that.

However you look at it though, any action we hope to inspire on the part of the prospect must be motivated by some kind of dissatisfaction with the consequence of what's presently happening or will happen in the prospect's world. And the concept of preventing loss is just as important as creating gain. Look at the insurance industry; its sole purpose is protecting you in case of loss. Somehow, they manage to present that as a positive, and you can, too.

Consequence questions make it easier for your prospects to see, hear, feel, and quantify the results of the current course of action, as compared to the change in direction that you are proposing. They

The Value Proposition Progression™
"The Key to Deal or No Deal"

Quadrant 3	Quadrant 2
Customer Doesn't Believe You Believe	Customer Believes You Believe
Deal Stalled	**Deal**
Quadrant 4	Quadrant 1
Customer Doesn't Believe You Don't Believe	Customer Thinks You Think
No Deal	**Start of Deal**

Figure 8.3

set the stage for the prospect to make a final decision about whether or not you have a deal.

Deal or No Deal?

The Value Proposition Progression™ helps us break down whether or not you are on your way to making a sale.

Notice that Figure 8.3 has four quadrants, each of which displays a different combination of the mindsets under which you and your potential client may be operating. Quadrant 1, in the bottom right-hand corner, represents the beginning of a deal. Based on the great work you did in generating interest through your Resource Proclamation and issues-based questions, both you and the customer THINK there is a basis for a potentially better outcome than what's happening right now in the prospect's world. As a result, the prospect gives you time and attention to explore the situation further and is willing to hear what you have to say.

If things go really well, you create an effective value proposition, which means that both you and the customer BELIEVE that your proposal actually provides a better outcome. That means you will progress to Quadrant 2 in the upper right-hand corner. This is the quadrant where you have a deal, and it is, of course, the destination you've been working so hard to reach. This is your payday.

But what happens if, after you flesh out the situation and make your pitch, your value proposition falls short? What happens if you are the only one who believes in your solution? Unfortunately, that does happen. Sometimes the deal stalls, and when this is the case, you will find yourself stuck in Quadrant 3 in the upper left-hand corner. This is where only the customer DOESN'T BELIEVE something should happen. and you still BELIEVE there's a reason to move forward. Here, you're more convinced than the customer is.

Is it possible to move out of Quadrant 3 and into Quadrant 2? Sure. Anything's possible. What you need to be aware of, though, is this: The more time you spend in Quadrant 3 trying to convince your customer to accept your proposal, the less profitable your deal becomes.

More resources spent inevitably results in less profit. And we are talking about all the resources that matter: time, personnel, money, and effort. From the point of view of time alone, the more time it takes you to close a deal, the less time you have to go after other deals.

The reason that you wind up in Quadrant 3 is that you have failed to create a value proposition that's compelling enough to convert your prospect into a believer. For some reason, you haven't done a good enough job of uncovering the consequences a customer faces as a result of not going with your solution. A classic reason for that, of course, is that you were too interested in talking about your features, and you never engaged the customer enough to get him or her sharing personal opinions about what's really at stake.

How often do you find yourself in Quadrant 3 struggling to make it into Quadrant 2? Probably more often than you'd like. With practice, you can reduce this time. Consistently asking the questions that will help you create and execute a powerful value proposition with your prospects really will reduce the total amount of time you spend in Quadrant 3.

As for the bottom left-hand corner of the diagram, that's Quadrant 4, the spot where neither you nor the customer believes in your solution. When you land there, of course, it is definitely time to move on.

Three Motivators

There are three main motivators that will drive prospects as they decide whether or not they should move forward with you. Inevitably, the consequence of not working with you must touch on some compelling reason to take action. That compelling reason must be fueled by one, two, or all three of these motivators.

1. *Tangible Motivators*

Many prospects and customers (especially those operating under the outcome-oriented mindset I shared with you in Chapter 4) will tell you, in essence, "Prove it. Show me the quantifiable results; show me the working model; show me the written guarantee. Show me something that is clearly, rationally, and logically connected to the outcome I want. I don't feel like taking any risks or going on your gut instincts—or anyone else's, for that matter. I want to be able to count it, hold it in my hands, and get a sense of absolute certainty. If you want to do business with me, you'd better prove what you're saying beyond the shadow of a doubt."

For the sake of argument, let's assume that the prospect's underlying concern—the tangible factor by which they're being motivated—is to raise revenues by 15 percent. When you're dealing with this kind of person, you have to ask yourself some tough questions: Can you show the prospect realistic, reliable projections of how much income your solution will actually produce? Will your solution help your customer reach his or her goal? Can you prove it, just as someone who reports to this person as an employee would have to do if she were proposing a major new undertaking? Are you willing to justify all your projections and even offer a backup scenario in which things don't turn out quite so well and your contact's organization still hits the target?

Or suppose that your contact is interested in getting proof about improved productivity. Can you tell this person how much increased productivity the organization can expect to enjoy as a result of working with you? Can you provide a realistic forecast of how much you're going to increase productivity and outline what you or your organization is going to do to follow up after the sale to make sure it happens exactly as you've promised?

People who are moved by tangible motivations want verifiable information. They may look at the decision process as being black-and-white and hard-nosed. If you can't quantify it, it's not realistic for this person. To appeal to this perception, you might say something like this: "We were able to increase production at Company X by 15 percent; this analysis shows what your program would look like if we were to improve production by 10 percent at your organization, which seems to be a realistic goal." That's tangible, and so is following up to make sure the increased production takes place as you've promised.

2. Intangible Motivators

Intangible motivators connect to things that you really can't quantify with hard numbers, but that nevertheless have a definite positive effect on the organization to which you're selling. Sometimes prospects and customers can't attach a dollar figure or a percentage value to what they want to get accomplished, but they still want to accomplish it. For instance, people may want to make sure that other people get a better overall feeling about their organization. That's a classic example of an intangible decision-making factor. Such factors could take the form of:

- Increased prestige within the industry
- Greater visibility
- Improved corporate image
- A better media relations strategy
- Better customer perceptions of the organization's ability to deliver quality or stand behind its products/services

Some prospects are naturally drawn to intangible factors; others need an outsider to highlight exactly what's at stake in this area. By appealing to a prospect's or customer's unspoken desire to see increases in various intangible areas, you can expand the parameters of a discussion.

Cost issues come to mind in such a situation. Often, when you're trying to sell superior products, there is a higher dollar cost, and you run into resistance from someone who says, "I simply can't afford to pay $100 per unit. I know your equipment will deliver the results we want, but the budget says $85 per unit. You're going to have to come down." That, of course, is a tangible factor concern. What sales leaders understand, however, is that if you ask the right issues-based question up front, you can highlight important intangible factor concerns as well and place the cost issues (or other tangible-factor hurdles) in perspective. Why? Because you know where the person is trying to go!

One of my clients sold film for X-ray machines, along with filmless imaging technology, to hospitals and imaging centers. Their goal was to convert as many customers as possible from buying film to purchasing the new filmless technology, which allows images to be stored permanently on computers with no need to print them out. Although radiologists don't have enough authority to make the final decision, they are nevertheless important buying influencers in this situation. When my client spoke to radiologists and asked what improvements they were looking for, many responded that they wanted "a better quality of life"; specifically, they wanted to be able to sleep through the night! Doctors were calling them at all hours to find out where the X-ray film and printouts were. That is, therefore, a compelling example of an intangible benefit the new system delivered; the doctor would always know where to find the image and would always be able to call it up without interrupting a radiologist's good night's sleep!

What kind of intangible benefits could you uncover? There are dozens—maybe hundreds—of possibilities; all you need to do is ask the right questions to the right people. For instance, you might ask early on in the interview, "What do you feel your organization represents to its customers? How do you want customers to perceive your company?" The prospect might answer, "Well, we want to give our customers the cutting-edge technology and the highest possible quality. That's what makes us superior to the competition."

Later on in the discussion, you can use a consequence question to highlight an important intangible factor. Perhaps the prospect balks at your catalog price. You might say, "Well, wait a second. What are the consequences if you don't match the objectives you've set about delivering cutting-edge technology to your customers? What happens if, because of this price problem, your product quality starts to drop? That might lead to some tradeoffs and to depreciation in the perceived value you offer your customers. What is that going to do? What are the consequences of failing to deliver that quality?" You've highlighted an important intangible factor that the prospect himself brought up: positive perception by customers in the marketplace.

Sales leaders learn to identify the intangible factors that are most important to their customers and connect them to tangible motivators. Let's say that the customer is spending $20 million on an intangible factor: that of projecting a certain image. That $20 million investment may be jeopardized if the customer's (intangible) image suffers due to inferior parts.

Perhaps that strategy sounds a little extreme to you. You should know, however, that it's turned around plenty of senior officers when delivered in a direct and accessible way. Such questioning focuses your prospect's attention on an important intangible factor and puts price issues in perspective. The higher up you go in the organization, the more likely you are to be able to make this kind of appeal effectively.

3. *Emotional Motivators*

Emotional decision-making motivators are rooted in your prospect's or customer's pride, sense of well-being, self-esteem, or other positive emotional state. Very often a purchase decision is in the result of a desire to avoid an unpleasant emotional experience and instead enjoy a positive one. Let's be realistic; sometimes purchase decisions are made because the buyer wants to make a statement to other people in the organization on a personal level or "show the competition a thing or two." These are clearly emotionally driven choices.

The perceived emotional value of a purchase leads someone to think along the following lines: "I don't need hard-number proof. I'm not trying to improve my company's image; I just deserve to have this, and I deserve to have it now." Emotional factors are often rooted in a desire to make a personal announcement to the world about one's own power and prestige. Some people view problems related to increasing profits, improving productivity, reducing costs, or gaining the competitive edge as deeply personal matters, and feel that they have something to prove. They are determined to surround themselves with the best no matter what, which means that, in some situations, the low cost for which other prospects are searching can actually be perceived as a drawback! You should always think twice before discounting, but you should definitely think twice when you're dealing with someone who places a premium on the emotional value of prestige purchases.

This is an inside game, which is another way of saying that emotional motivators are not the same as intangible motivators. Intangible factors have to do with external concerns like market share, image, and perception by customers. Emotional factors, on the other hand, are always connected to a prospect's internal concerns.

Now, from a certain angle, all of our purchase decisions say something about who we are to the outside world, and so there is at least some element of emotion to virtually every sale. Consider, for instance, that advertisers spend millions of dollars convincing people that the brand of toothpaste or cologne that they buy will have a major impact on the quality of their social or family life. There's an old saying in sales, one that's just as valid today as it was 50 years ago: "Whenever you begin to get interested in something, the interest starts with the heart." That's as strong a description of the role emotional factors play in selling as I've ever heard. In some situations, emotions play not just an important role, but the dominant role.

In the county where I live in New Jersey, there's a classic tale that illustrates the role that emotional motivators can play in purchase decisions. A Fortune 500 executive supposedly built a house that was designed to be the biggest house in that executive's neighborhood. A few years went by and, lo and behold, somebody else built a bigger house on the same street. The executive, peeved that he no longer had the biggest house in the area, built a duplicate of his first house and had it connected to the original dwelling! Now he definitely had the biggest house on the block again. (And some contractors were doubtless very happy about that.) I wouldn't have believed that such a house even existed if I hadn't seen it with my own eyes.

Here was a decision that was purely driven by a desire to attain a certain status within the community: "I'm going to have the *biggest* house on the block!" Lots of purchase decisions, large and small, are driven by much the same outlook: "I'm going to buy a cherry-red Porsche; I deserve it." "I'm going to make the biggest splash of anyone at the party; I need the swankiest dress in your store."

Prospect: "I'm going to have the number-one department in the company, no matter what."

Recruiter: "In that case, you're going to want the best people available!"

If you can appeal effectively to these motivations, you can land the business.

Of course, once this decision is made, people are still going to try to beat you up on price and get the best terms. But imagine how strong you could be in presenting and defending your core value proposition if you knew what was really behind the original decision to buy!

What's the Compelling Reason?

Your Consequence Question must point your prospect to a compelling reason to take action—a reason that connects to at least one, and preferably all three, of the possible driving motivations you just read about. Look once again at the example I shared with you a little earlier in this chapter:

> "Let me ask you this: Are you really willing to sacrifice a solution that we've established will get you to the $2 million in operating cost reductions that your CEO is looking for, improve your customer's experience, and keep you from having to lay off 20 people . . . all because of an $80,000 difference in price?"

Does this touch on tangible motivators? Yes, that's the $2 million in operating cost reductions. What about intangible motivators? Those are there too: we're out to improve the "customer's experience," which is something that's definitely important and often very difficult to measure. How about emotions? Would you say that there's any emotional motivator in play when we talk about delivering something the CEO has declared to be a priority for all the company's department heads? Absolutely! After all, we're assuming that the prospect wants to keep the CEO happy and hold on to his job!

The compelling reason to take action here connects to all three motivators. The sum total of the consequences you uncover should always connect to at least one of those motivators so that you can make the case for the prospect to continue moving forward with you. If the consequences link to these motivators—and if they're based on things the prospect has told you (as opposed to things you have told the prospect)—then you will move into Quadrant 2 instead of getting stuck in Quadrant 3!

Remember, only the customer's opinion of whether or not you have provided enough of a compelling reason to change is important. Your opinion about any of this simply does not matter. That's why you want to expand the dialogue and use the early stage of the sales cycle to uncover as many consequences as possible. You don't want to fall short later on in the discussion.

Case Study: Kodak

When it comes to building a solid value proposition, you can find a lot less effective places to begin than identifying something your buyer absolutely hates about their current situation. Imaging giant Kodak, for example, understood that the number one thing consumers hated about printing at home was the high price of ink.

Kodak gleaned this important information by surveying consumers and finding out that more than 80 percent of people who print at home identified the price of ink as their primary dissatisfaction. Kodak uncovered some amazing stories on this score: stories about parents hiding ink from their children to keep them from printing too much, parents hiding the printer itself from the children, and even people throwing away their printers because the ink cartridges were too expensive and buying another printer altogether!

What was giving consumers fits was the way the industry had decided to sell inkjet printers and components. The traditional way to market inkjet printers is to sell the printer at a significant loss and make up the profit later on ink sales. This causes people who don't print very often to simply buy a new, cheap printer with ink tanks included instead of spending $70 or more on the cartridges alone.

After hearing from its patrons, Kodak had a clear indication of the significant emotional toll all that expensive ink was having on customers. In response, the company took a leadership position by developing a revolutionary new business approach. Kodak launched a new line of all-in-one inkjet printers in 2006, and in doing so, launched a new way of thinking about printers.

Kodak's All-in-One printers, while competitively priced, are not the cheapest printers on the market. They are easy-to-use machines that produce extremely high-quality prints at roughly half the cost of ink when compared to traditional inkjet printers. In the United States, the cost of Kodak's ink was $9.99 for black ink, as compared to up to $19.99 for competitors' black ink cartridges—and $14.99 for a five-ink color cartridge, as compared to up to $57 for competitors' color ink cartridges! This significant inconvenience of frequently changing print cartridges combined with the actual high cost of inkjet cartridges makes up the cost of the no change (CNC) portion of the equation for Kodak's All-in-One inkjet printers.

The All-in-One Value Proposition

Here's Kodak's value proposition for its All-in-One printer. It involves a comparison of the cost of ink over two years based on average usage of a competing model instead of the Kodak printer.

Cost of no change minus cost of change equals perceived value or $CNC - CC = PV$.

CNC ($450 in additional ink expenses over the course of two years + emotional cost) − CC ($150 price for mid-range Kodak printer) = PV ($300 cash + significant emotional relief + not having to invest the time and effort to hide the ink and/or the printer from the kids).

This formula only works in the salesperson's favor if the CNC (cost of no change) is *significantly* higher than the CC (cost of change). The buyer has to have a compelling enough reason to go through the trouble and expense of changing!

Kodak's Strategic Plan

There have been a lot of changes in Kodak's industry since the company's inception in 1892. Its role has been significantly altered compared to what it was just a few years ago. Kodak's key differentiator as a company, which lies at the crossroads of materials science and digital imaging.

Kodak has been for decades—and remains—the world leader in imaging. The company's technology is incorporated into nearly every digital camera on the market today. In addition, Kodak has more than a century's experience in applying chemicals and inks to paper and other substrates—from developing photographic prints to high-speed electrophotographic and commercial inkjet printers. That's a fancy way of saying that the technology that made its All-In-One series of printers possible wasn't new to Kodak. The company simply decided to take its strategic brand promise of ease of use and trustworthiness and apply it to the business proposition of consumer inkjet printers. The outcome—saving people up to 50 percent on everything they print compared to similar inkjet printers—was both revolutionary and in line with Kodak's strategic plan.

As Kodak's Chief Business Development Officer Jeffrey Hayzlett told me, "The New Kodak is composed of a growing digital franchise and a sustainable traditional imaging business. . . . Kodak's strategy is to compete in those markets where we can take advantage of our unmatched combination of imaging science and materials science, such as our new efforts in inkjet printing, among many others."

The Value Is in the Mix

There are five main areas where you can take a cue from Kodak and add value to your prospect's or customer's world. As evidenced by the imaging company's longevity and variety of service, the question is not what one area will win the sale for you, but how you can create a unique mix from these five value areas to create a total package or a unique mixture that appeals to your prospect in a specific way. Take a look at the five value elements now, and notice that your product or service is only one of them.

- *Information.* This includes pieces like your web resources, e-newsletter, and product/service updates—whether they are delivered by "snail mail" or via e-mail or text message. Information also encompasses the knowledge that you or someone in your organization has about current events and trends in the prospect's or customer's industry. Remember, industry trends, forecasts, and recommendations are items of high value to customers!
- *Distribution.* This is your organization's ability to get a product, or anything else, from point A to point B. Distribution can affect a customer's business by means of speed of delivery and by your ability to deliver often and reduce a customer's inventory loads, to give just two examples.

- *Systems.* This is your organization's ability to support your customers and streamline their buying process. If you operate an e-commerce site, or any form of Internet- or Intranet-based order placement and confirmation, that falls under systems.
- *Assets for Key Customers.* This is your organization's ability to provide your best customers with critical technical, financial, and interpersonal resources. Basically, these are the ethically and legally sound outcomes you know you have to find a way to deliver in order to hold onto your most important accounts.
- *Product/Service.* Notice that your organization's ability to set up and implement superior solutions is only *one* of the five value areas.

Now ask yourself this: If two parties are perceived to be selling the exact same product or service, how will one differentiate itself over the other? If you said "by cutting prices," go to the back of the class! The differentiation is in the mix. For example, one of my clients offered tele-metering for their customers; in essence, they give their clients electronic systems for keeping tabs on inventory, and when the product gets down to a certain point the system generates an order automatically. This allows customers to improve operations in such areas as just-in-time inventory, elimination of stock-outs, and on-time delivery. Up to this point, the customer's product features were exactly the same as the competition's. What I helped my client do was enhance the value of the mix by customizing their systems to improve the distribution process and make better utilization of inventories. This, in turn, created a mix that delivered a better result to the end user—on-time or even early delivery. That translated to improved customer satisfaction levels for my client's customers, which was something the client wasn't getting from the competition and something they were trying to improve!

Take the Time, Make It Unique

Creating a unique value proposition has only two drawbacks: You must treat individual prospects like (are you ready?) individuals and you must abandon the myth that one size fits all when it comes to issuing compelling reasons to act. Sales leaders have no problem whatsoever taking the time to connect with prospects as individuals, and they have no problem making the reasons they offer to take action unique to that prospect's situation. Follow their lead: listen, ask the right questions, and develop a value proposition that is compelling enough to motivate your prospect to take action and move the sales process forward.

Your Chapter Eight Commitment

Think back on a sale you lost. Did you make your presentation, demonstration, or recommendation too early? What could you have asked the prospect about that you didn't ask? Knowing what you know now, what value proposition could you have created for this person?

What percentage of your selling time would you estimate you now spend in Quadrant 2 of the value progression? What percentage of your selling time do you spend in Quadrant 3?

Once you've completed these activities, list three things that you are committed to doing to improve your value proposition so you spend less time in Quadrant 3 and more time in Quadrant 2.

 # COMMITMENT!

(Pronunciation: ko-'mit-mint, Function: noun, Definition: a: an agreement or pledge to do something in the future; b: something pledged c: the state or an instance of being obligated or emotionally impelled, a commitment to a cause)

_____

_____

_____

_____

_____

_____

_____

_____

_____

_____

_____

_____

_____

_____

_____

_____

_____

_____

_____

_____

For more of these sample sheets go to http://www.leadsellorgetoutoftheway.com.

Figure 8.4   Commitment Sheet

9 | Communicating Persuasively

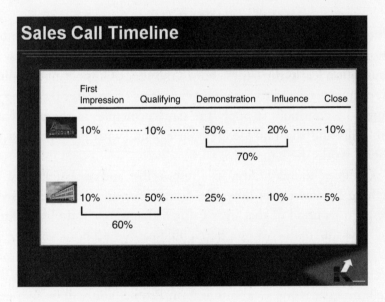

Figure 9.1

You are moving into the demonstration/influence phase! If you've done your work properly up to this point, both you and the prospect are ready to move on to the specific recommendation that will address the issues you have uncovered and show exactly how your products and services will meet the prospect's challenges.

> ### The Leader's Advantage
>
> Leaders communicate so persuasively about both the issues and the vision that they *bring the future into the present*.

Your Communications MBA

I think of this part of the book as your MBA in persuasive communications. Someone who completes an advanced degree in business administration learns the basics about a number of important disciplines and strategies related to running a business. Then, after receiving the degree, he continues to apply the same principles in the real world. The skills and the knowledge base expand with practice, and this chapter works the same way.

I've tried to synthesize, in a responsible and accessible way, everything I know about how sales leaders communicate persuasively. I've tried to fit all of that into a single chapter even though I know that the topic I am covering here could easily be a book this size. (In fact, what I discuss in this chapter could be several books!) But once you become familiar with the basic principles of the complex of skills I call the Leadership Communication Profile, you will be in a good position to expand your capacity with practice out in the real world. This is something you're going to get better at by doing over time, but it's not something you're going to master by reading a chapter in a book.

Improving your Leadership Communication Profile is a lifelong effort. You will never be finished improving yourself in this area.

Low-Impact Presentations Deliver Low-Impact Commissions

Sales leaders deliver powerful presentations that land with high impact and that persuade people to take action. Sales followers, on the other hand, deliver low-impact presentations—presentations that land with a whimper and leave people saying, "Let us think it over." The Leadership Communication Profile is the complex set of communication abilities that make "Let us think it over" a thing of the past.

I've worked with thousands of salespeople, including some of the very best in the country, and I can assure you that expanding and upgrading your Leadership Communication Profile is imperative if you really intend to perform at the top level.

Here's something else that I've learned over the years: In any given organization, there are some professional salespeople who plateau—that is, who reach a certain point in their career and personal income potential and then simply hit the wall. They cannot seem to get beyond a certain point in their career. Most or all of those salespeople stopped working on their own personal development; they stopped setting new goals and trying to improve themselves. They settled for the selling strategies they were used to—*because* they were used to them.

My assumption is that you don't fall into that category because (a) you picked up this book and started reading it, which means you're focused on improving yourself and moving forward in your career; and (b) you've made it all the way through to this chapter, which suggests to me that you are actively looking for the very best communication tools you can find. My assumption is that you genuinely want to keep moving forward in your career. This attitude is something that sets you apart from other salespeople. Most are actually fearful of moving forward to the next level.

There may be certain aspects of sales communications that your peers find especially intimidating, such as giving a speech before a trade group or a gathering of prospects (even though such a speech presents awesome prospecting opportunities). Or they may be nervous about positioning themselves as experts in a group setting. Or they may worry about setting forth a clear set of comparisons that's based on what they themselves have learned about the consequences that face a prospect or a group of prospects, Or they may be reluctant to communicate *as a leader* to other leaders. Or, they may be uncomfortable speaking in a way that commands and expects respect, visibility, and attention from both individuals and groups.

Move Forward Anyway

The Leader's Wisdom

"It's natural to have butterflies. The secret is to get them to fly in formation."—Walter Cronkite

It's time for a reality check: Fear is part of the human experience.

Leaders accept that and then face the fear directly and take action anyway. For instance, as I mentioned, a lot of people are apprehensive about speaking in front of groups. You'd be surprised to learn how many truly great professional speakers out there experience stage fright but have simply developed good internal strategies for moving forward anyway. I've learned that some of my most admired role models go through this on a regular basis!

There was a point in my career when I would become incredibly nervous before some of the talks I was supposed to give. I started doing a little ritual for myself when I noticed that this was beginning to happen: I would sit myself down, breathe deeply, and ask myself, "What am I here for? What is the audience here for?" The answer I came up with was that the audience was there to get some ideas on how they can sell and lead more effectively. Then I would ask myself, "Do you have any of those ideas?" And the answer was always "Yes." Then I would say to myself, "Just go out and tell your story, and be there for the audience." And I'd be ready to go, back in a customer-focused mode instead of in a self-focused mode. Ultimately, that's all you want to do: tell your story while making sure that you are fully present for the audience.

The Leader's Advantage

You will know when you are self-focused before a presentation, because you will be extremely concerned about whether—and how—you will be judged by the audience. You may even talk yourself into believing that the only way the meeting will go well is if you give the best presentation the audience has ever heard. That's an impossible standard, of course, one that puts immense pressure on you and is likely to make you feel nervous. When you go back to being customer focused, however, you'll be thinking about the content people want and need to hear from you.

What follows will require you to cross the line that separates followers from leaders when it comes to delivering presentations. While some of what you read may seem like second nature to you, some of it may seem a little strange. If you find yourself looking at something that's unfamiliar, consider the following wise words from World War I flying ace Eddie Rickenbacker—words that I believe should be part of every sales leader's creed.

The Leader's Wisdom

"Courage is doing what you're afraid to do. There can be no courage unless you're scared." —Eddie Rickenbacker

The Leadership Communication Profile

The Leadership Communication Profile comprises seven critical skills, each of which intersects with and supports the other six skills. The skills are not a sequence for you to follow when you present; they are a set of interlocking principles that will enable you to deliver a fantastic presentation or demonstration.

Your goal should be to fully master all seven principles, but you definitely don't have to wait for that to happen before you deliver a presentation. All you have to do is choose to be one of those rare people who make continuous improvement in all seven a daily reality in your life. No great leader—in sales or any other endeavor—rises to the top without executing on these seven skill areas on a consistent basis when delivering sales presentations . . . or any kind of presentation. The seven skills are:

1. Establishing Congruence
2. Assessing the Audience and the Opportunity

3. Translating
4. Making Them Laugh
5. Giving Options
6. Supporting the Message with the Medium (Not Vice Versa)
7. Resolving Conflicts

Skill #1: Establishing Congruence

Congruence is simply authentic communication based that sincerely conveys your ultimate message: namely, that you mean—and are fully invested in—what you have to say and that you assume full personal responsibility for the position you are laying out in your presentation. To use a more common phrase, congruence means that you walk your talk. It means you have enough energy and drive to be genuinely enthusiastic about the topic you're discussing because you are passionate about it and believe in it.

Establishing congruence is the starting point of any effective presentation. If the person or group to whom you're speaking is not convinced that you actually mean what you say and are willing to stand behind it, they will tune out. And they should!

Some people will tell you that establishing congruence is all about delivering the right message with your body language and tone. They'll try to convince you that standing and speaking in a certain way will establish your congruence for the people to whom you're talking. While it's certainly true that body language and vocal tonality have a huge effect on your ability to establish congruence with someone, elaborate "congruence checklists" that people put together tend to make the person who's delivering the presentation too tense about whether he or she is following all the right steps, standing the right way, and talking the right way. And when you're tensed up about whether you're standing and talking the way you're supposed to, can you guess what that does for the congruence level of your message? The congruence actually drops. People can tell that you're distracted by something, and they assume there's something inconsistent and insincere about your message. They don't know that you're stressed out because you're trying to remember the list of things to do; they think it's because you don't really believe what you're saying, and you're nervous that this is about to be discovered in public.

Put aside the long lists that tell you how to stand, how to walk, and how to speak. At the end of the day, congruence simply means being 100 percent present for your prospects and not pretending you know something when you don't. Your job is actually very simple: be yourself.

My friend Sam Silverstein, who, as of this writing, is the president of the National Speakers Association, chose a theme for his one-year tenure that fits this subject perfectly: "Keep It Real." It's hard for me to think of a time when three simple English words packed so much meaning or were so relevant to the issue of leadership communications. Yes, there is a time and a place for in-depth presentation training, and you can definitely gain a lot from taking a program like that from a qualified pro. At the same time, you don't have to wait until you have mastered such a program before you give a presentation!

Until you can internalize all the great skills waiting to be learned about tone, body language, timing, and the rest of it, simply focus on being yourself. Focus on congruence and on keeping it real. Do so on a regular basis, get good at it, and you will have the first skill—establishing congruence—down cold. Keep it real no matter what. Don't try to talk over people's heads or be someone you're not. Don't try to tap-dance your way around problems if they come up. Just look people in the eye and connect, person-to-person, about what you really believe deep down inside.

Did You Hear the Story About ...?

Stories are an essential tool in your presentation. They help you to illustrate your points and connect with your audience. When crafted and delivered correctly, they build trust, acceptance, and authenticity. The right stories can be a major asset when you are trying to establish congruence.

Throughout this book I've shared anecdotes with you that illustrate one or more of the leadership selling strategies I've discussed. I've done so because stories—especially those that are true and that come from the narrator's direct experience—have a way of building power and impact into any lesson. That's as true for a presentation as it is for a book about selling. People love stories, especially those that engage the mind and emotions. When a leader starts telling a story that everyone in the room starts relating it to personal experience, and that's exactly what you want!

Testimonials are a specific kind of story, a very powerful one about how real people have experienced real solutions as a result of working with you. They can be extremely influential, as long as they are verifiable! Don't make things up, and don't pass along accounts that you aren't sure about. Get your contact's permission before using his or her name and company affiliation in a success story. This is both ethically sound and pragmatic, because you want this person to know that he or she is likely to be called by your prospects. If you can't get the person to agree to take calls from prospects, but the events of the story are accurate and the person doesn't mind you passing them along, tell a version that gets the essence of the point across, but that doesn't name names or company affiliations.

Whenever possible, try to give accounts that arise from direct personal experience. These will always leave a stronger impact than stories you pass along from a third party. Remember, whatever you are selling, there are probably a dozen other people who are selling something comparable. People will buy from you because of your unique insights and experiences, . . . and nothing gets that across like a powerful story you can tell in the first person or the "I" voice.

Skill #2: Assessing the Audience and the Opportunity

True sales leaders never simply start the presentation. They open with a grabber of some kind—a bold statement intended to move the audience and win attention and interest. This might even mean making the audience feel uncomfortable about something. For instance:

> "Good morning. Over the past two weeks, we have spoken to several people in this room, and we have identified areas where Acme Company can significantly improve its cash flow and its competitive advantage in the marketplace. This ties into some of the key objectives that your CEO shared in his message to you last week, and, as he put it then, 'Failure is not an option.' Today, we are going to share some simple strategies on how you can improve the cash flow picture within 90 days, enhance your competitive advantage among end-users, and extend the legacy and life of a company that started doing business in 1888."

In the above statement, the audience will feel just a little uncomfortable because of the reminder that changes are necessary if they intend to stay in business. The opening statement points to a positive outcome with a Resource Proclamation of how this meeting is going to provide dramatic solutions to the issues of the day. As a result, everyone's on board. The presentation can begin.

Sales leaders know that this "buy-in" moment must happen before they launch into their presentation. No matter how much time, energy, and attention they may have put into preparing it, and no matter whether they've been waiting all week, all month, or all year to start talking, they take a moment before they begin the presentation to win attention, deliver a brief overview of the meeting's purpose, and then gauge two very important factors: the audience and the opportunity. These two factors can and do change without a moment's notice.

Leaders know that every audience is going to be different based on things like who's in attendance, what time of day it is, how long it's been since people have eaten, what happened right before the meeting, and so on. Even if you're talking to precisely the same people you talked to last week, you can find yourself dealing with a totally different ambience and emotional outlook, and thus a totally different level of engagement. A great presenter will always take the audience's temperature so that he or she can figure out what pacing, tonality, and timeframe is appropriate for the audience. (I'll share some temperature-taking strategies with you in just a moment.)

In addition, sales leaders know that every opportunity is different, and they know that the opportunity around which they built their presentation may have changed dramatically since the last time the leader connected with this audience. As a result, they never march lockstep through a presentation. If the circumstances have changed, then the presentation has to change, no matter how much or how little preparation has gone into it.

Let's look at each of these two activities—assessing the audience and the opportunity—in depth.

Assessing the Audience

Assessing the audience is an essential skill. I don't care whether you're presenting to two people or 200; you can't begin your act until you've found some way to connect with each and every member of your audience and convinced each one that this meeting really is worth paying attention to. You want *them* to see that what you have to say is going to get them where they want to go.

After you've won the audience's attention, you might continue with a statement like, "We've done a lot of work to get ready for this meeting, and we've prepared some materials for you to look at today. But before we get started, please help me out by helping me to answer this question: If this meeting were to be as successful today as you want it to be, what issues would you need it to cover?"

Work your way around the room to find out the answers. Write them down on a flipchart or a whiteboard or, if you don't have access to either of those, keep track of each issue raised and the name of the person who raised it. So, for instance, when you get to the audience member named Bill, and Bill says his top issue he needs the meeting to cover is security, you write down "BILL—SECURITY" in great big letters. Continue the process of recording each audience member's key issue(s) until you've covered everyone. By the way, this is the approach to use if you're presenting before a comparatively small group of people—say, five or fewer. When dealing with larger groups, ask the same question, get a single person's response, write down the person's name, and then ask for a show of hands to illustrate how many people feel that that's a key concern. Make sure you uncover all issues that are of concern to the people in the room.

You are, of course, asking this question and recording all this information for a reason: The answers to the questions you are posing must serve as the framework for the presentation you deliver. Later on, *after* you've assessed the opportunity and you've begun your presentation in earnest, you're going to reach a point in your presentation that connects to each person's issue. So when you get to the part that connects to Bill's issue—security—you're going to stop where you are, go back to your list, and say something like this: "This brings us to security, which was an important issue that Bill raised before we got started."

This next part is extremely important—don't skip over it! Make eye contact directly with Bill, and focus on him—and only him—as you explore the issue he raised. Begin to engage directly with Bill by saying, "Bill, let me tell you why I think security is such an important issue, and how we're proposing that it be addressed. . . ." (Then continue with all the best information and insight you have on the topic that is near and dear to Bill's heart.)

At this point, I have to share a presentation secret: Every person in the room will feel a close connection with you, and will feel as though you have been talking directly to him or her personally, simply because you are focusing all of your attention closely on Bill as you cover his issue. If you covered exactly the same content while pacing back and forth, without engaging with Bill or anyone else, it wouldn't land with impact for Bill as an individual or for your audience as a group. You'd be spraying your message all over the place! The goal is not simply to deliver the content, but to make sure that the message lands with impact for each and every person in the room.

If you have addressed the topic completely and if you can tell from body language or direct engagement with Bill that he is satisfied with what you've shared with him about security, then you're ready to move on. But don't just continue to the next issue in a rush. Pause for a moment and let your exchange with Bill register for the whole room.

In professional speaker's parlance, this critical pause is known as "landing the point," and it's an extremely important part of the process. There is one caveat for you to consider before you use it. If you are giving an explanation to Bill that is rather long, you obviously don't want to stare at Bill all that time and make him feel uncomfortable. Simply acknowledge him for bringing the issue up, present a point, let it land, and move to another person or part of the room for the second point relating to the same issue.

The Leader's Advantage

You can prove the power of the "landing the point" strategy any time you want. Call the family together or gather a few friends. Quickly say one or two sentences with your focus darting all over the place, without making eye contact with anyone; make sure you rush from point to point. Now, say the same words again. But this time focus on one person when you are talking, and pause before you move on to your next point. I guarantee you that if you do the experiment correctly, you will see a huge difference in the way your message is received.

Continue in this manner with each issue raised by each audience member at the outset of the session. Your presentation will not be complete until the entire audience, and each individual member, concludes that they got what they came for.

Assessing the audience properly—and following through on that assessment as you deliver your presentation and shape it to the group's needs—means shifting from self-focus mode to customer-focus mode. This is something sales leaders do intuitively. You'll never see a true sales leader get hung up in a list of questions, or obsess about following a series of pre-established points exactly as they've been laid out in a PowerPoint deck. Instead, you'll see the sales leader adapting his or her issues to the concerns of the audience and connecting one-on-one with each individual who's raised an issue or concern.

Assessing the Opportunity

Now, what about the other half of this equation: assessing the opportunity?

The best presentations are conversations, not performances. And you can't possibly have a conversation with someone if both parties haven't agreed on what to talk about! So here's the scenario you want to avoid: You walk in, shake hands, engage in a little small talk, and work your way through that beautiful presentation you created last week, the one with all the bells and whistles and flashy animations. You do a great job of presenting the material. Everyone agrees on that much. You get a round of applause! But you don't get the deal.

Why not? Well, because last night—before you even began the presentation—the agenda changed. Your main contact at the company was fired, and a new decision maker was put in place. That new decision maker has put everything on hold; all purchasing initiatives from the multi-million-dollar software and training package you're proposing, all the way down to the $1.49 box of paper clips people would use to hold copies of your proposal together. All proceedings in this department must now wait until the new decision maker gets his bearings, which could take anywhere from two days to two months. When you finally do meet this person, you will be starting from scratch. You just wasted an hour of your life delivering a great presentation just to be informed that you'll have to start all over again at some later point in time—maybe next month, maybe next quarter, who knows. That's not how leaders invest their time!

In the situation above, the most obvious change is the change in decision makers. But are there other changes going on, changes that you may not be privy to or simply do not find out about unless you ask? You need to find out so that you don't waste your time and so that you can adjust your presentation accordingly.

Don't make this more complicated than it actually is. All you really have to do is ask something like this: "Have there been any changes I should know about since our last conversation?" If there have been, you'll want to use the session to start taking notes again and strategize your best next move with the people in the room.

Assess the opportunity first and you'll find it much, much easier to start and sustain a dialogue that benefits both sides during your presentation.

The Perfect Assessment

Earlier in this book, I told you the story of a client of mine who manufactures film for the radiology industry. As you may recall, the account executives were undertaking a technology conversion by moving their hospital accounts and imaging centers from film-based systems to filmless systems. Of course, there were a lot of stakeholders involved in that decision, including everyone from the radiologists who worked with the equipment to the doctors who used the images, to the administrators in the hospital who approve major purchases and compare vendors. What you may not have realized, however—and what I didn't know until my client told me—was that this group of stakeholders also included the people who often end up being the real decision makers: the benefactors who must decide whether to pony up the money for a new system. In this case, it was a group of key financial contributors to the hospital, mostly women above the age of 50. My client came to me and asked for help developing the presentation for this group. Would I take a look at his PowerPoint presentation? Of course, I was happy to do so.

When I saw the slides he was planning to show this group of older folks, I nearly fell over. He had maybe 40 slides in his presentation, and 35 of them dealt with the technical specifications and capacities of the equipment. Remember, he was preparing to deliver a talk before a group of very wealthy people, mostly women who were between 50 and 85 years of age. These people were probably just as eager to get to the point as a roomful of CEOs, and they probably weren't waiting with bated breath to hear all about the technical ins and outs of these machines.

I told him, "Look, you're dealing with a big group—50 people. Why don't you tell them you've got a lot of technical information about the system that would probably bore them to death and then spend some time asking these people about their experiences *as patients* with the X-ray technologies their doctors are using on them right now? Then you can take whatever problems show up and show them how the filmless system addresses each of those issues."

And that's how he designed the presentation. Instead of launching into a long lecture about the design of his company's technology, he asked the group what their personal experience with X-ray technology was. Using the group assessment process I shared with you earlier, he got answers like these:

- "I hate carrying big envelopes of film to my doctor's office."
- "I hate having to come back again because the doctor doesn't yet have the X-rays ready."
- "I hate having to wait a long time for results."

And so on. He spent about 10 minutes up front developing the real-world issues that each potential benefactor for the system had experienced in their own lives. Then he spent the rest of the session showing exactly how his company's filmless system would improve the outcomes for the benefactors themselves and every other patient requiring X-ray work.

He closed a multi-million-dollar deal as a result of that presentation 45 minutes after he concluded his meeting!

Skill #3: Translating the Message

Leaders know that the simple act of speaking the words that reflect their message is not enough to land that message with the audience.

The communication process is more complex than that, as the following graphic illustrates:

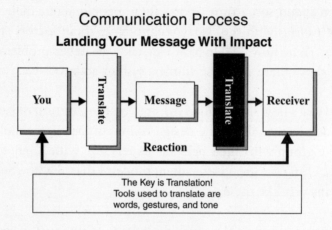

Communication Process
Landing Your Message With Impact

Figure 9.2

Notice that there's a "feedback loop" in place: The communication process starts when you translate the message you have in your mind into the words, gestures, and tonality that you believe support your message; then the individual members of the audience translate your message, based on their own past experiences, values, and assumptions, in an attempt to determine your intent. You then gauge the reaction you receive from your audience, and you start the process all over again. Notice, too, that you don't simply recite a performance that you've memorized ahead of time, but instead you constantly engage and re-engage with your audience by repeatedly asking yourself, "Have I landed this point?"

Your success in this effort depends upon your ability to send the appropriate verbal, visual, and body-language messages about the intent of your presentation. You'll recall that the very first skill we discussed in this chapter was the skill of establishing congruence. There is a significant overlap between congruence and translation, because that communication skill helps you translate your intent to the members of your audience.

The Leader's Advantage

Intent, then content, is what counts! The right content without the right intent often leads to the audience receiving the wrong message.

The people you're delivering your presentation to are always going to be asking themselves one powerful, unspoken question: "What is this person really after?" If the answer they get from your words, your gestures, and your tone is that you're after some short-term gain that's likely to come at their expense, but that you're trying to disguise that fact, your intended message will not land. As a result, you must constantly assess the audience's reaction to your message and regularly reorient yourself to your larger purpose—the purpose that connects, with both emotion and integrity, to the benefits the audience is likely to experience from working with you.

To give just one example of this kind of leadership communication from the world of politics, let me ask you to consider the presidential election of 1992, in which Bill Clinton, an obscure governor from a small state, defeated a sitting president, George H.W. Bush, who had recently led a successful war against a foreign aggressor. How did Clinton pull it off? Not by sending the message that he was highly ambitious and craved the power and privilege of the White House.

Instead, he successfully persuaded voters that his intent was to address their economic challenges because he himself understood the difficulties they were going through. That was his message! He did a better job of translating that message to individual voters, over the course of the campaign, than President Bush did. The phrase "I feel your pain," which Clinton actually said, became a catchphrase of the campaign. As a matter of history, "I feel your pain" landed Clinton's message and resonated with his audience. Voters were looking for someone who felt their pain. Clinton did a better job, in any given speech or event, of managing the feedback loop with his audiences than Bush did with his own version of the "I feel your pain" message. As a result, Clinton was able to land that message more effectively than Bush.

Whether you were a fan of Clinton's policies or not, you should take some time to assess his awe-inspiring translation skills. Your goal as a leader is the same as Clinton's was in 1992: to land your message and stimulate your prospects into a new thinking process, to engage them about the issues that are important to them, and to translate your message in such a way that it actually connects with your intended audience on a deeply personal and emotional level. If your presentation doesn't get people either talking or thinking (and you can easily tell if this is the case by monitoring their body language), then you've got a problem. In all likelihood, one of two things is happening: either you yourself are not clear on the purpose that should be driving your message, or you are not translating your message effectively and not managing the feedback loop as a sales leader.

It takes time and practice to master the art of translation, and it requires that you become acutely aware of the verbal and non-verbal reactions you receive. Raise your point, but don't stop there. Start a dialogue by listening to what the person on the other side of the conversation is telling you. Address your counterpart's issues and concerns, and before you dash on to the next point, maintain contact and remember the power of pausing to reinforce your message and intent before you leave the scene of the dialogue. Remember, pausing helps you land your point. As a rule of thumb, the bigger the point is, the longer the pause should be. We are talking about only seconds here, not minutes. The more closely you can focus on the audience member's body language and facial expression, the better the picture you will have of the person's internal translation of your message, and the clearer it will be to you whether you can move on safely.

The Leader's Advantage

If you do not notice and adjust to your audience's reaction, you will not be able to translate your message or land your underlying intent effectively. Gauge group reactions carefully, and don't overreact. One person yawning might mean the person didn't sleep well last night; five or 10 people yawning probably means you're not engaging people and need to change course. Another potentially dangerous sign is people sending lots of text messages. I recently watched someone deliver a presentation where half the audience was sending electronic notes as the speaker was talking. I did a little investigating, and saw for myself that many of these messages were about how boring the presentation was!

Here's a final piece of advice on translating your message: Find some way to change the physical surroundings if they aren't supporting your efforts to engage with the group. If the room is stiflingly hot, for instance, you must find some way to get the air conditioning on so that people can actually focus in on what you're saying—rather than on how uncomfortable they are.

Skill #4: Making Them Laugh

Let's face it. The act of purchasing can be stressful. People really don't know whether they are doing the right thing. They're about to decide whether or not to spend a lot of money, and they don't want to make a mistake. When people are in this nerve-racking state of mind, it's hard to build up a conversation with them and figure out how to effectively translate what you're doing.

Leaders know that appropriate humor makes the job of presentation much easier. In fact, humor changes everything. Stress is reduced. Endorphins are released in the brain, and people start to feel differently about the relationship you're establishing with them. It's not an accident that the greatest leaders know how to put a room or an individual contact at ease by producing a laugh.

If you can find a way to lighten the atmosphere, you will help your customers hear and understand the value you truly have to offer. But here's the tricky part: This is not merely a matter of telling jokes. Leaders find appropriate opportunities for relevant humor, typically on the spot and in real time. That's an art, not a science, and again, it's a topic that probably deserves a book-length discussion. In the limited space I have, I can only share the point that humor in presentations is an essential part of the dialogue, that it's definitely not the same as being a stand-up comic, and that some of the key opportunities for humor will become obvious to you only with practice.

The best and simplest example of this that I can give you is the principle of leading the conversation—or taking full control of it—by introducing something unexpected. This idea comes from my colleague Rory Vaden, who does a superb job of teaching sales executives how to integrate the art of humor into their sales presentations. Rory tells the story of a realtor who heard him speak and later sent him a testimonial after using this technique of introducing something unexpected.

The realtor was showing an investor an extremely nice piece of property, and the time had come for her to tell the investor how much it cost. The asking price was $1.2 million, and the realtor knew that it was indeed a fair price, given the quality of the property. As the words were coming out of her mouth, however, she could tell from the sudden changes in the investor's body language that he was uncomfortable. In a split-second, she made an on-the-spot improvisation. Here's what she ended up saying:

"The price is $1.2 million . . . and 27 cents!"

Her comment changed the emotional environment completely. The investor laughed out loud. The realtor had used Rory's concept of leading the conversation and ending with something the prospect never expected. Because of these tactics, she closed the deal!

Notice that the humor she used was spontaneous and appropriate to the situation. It put the realtor in a position to lead the conversation, and it put something on the table—27 cents—that the prospect absolutely didn't expect.

Of course, you can prepare some comments ahead of time; I certainly do. And that is quite different from blurting out a joke that has absolutely nothing to do with the relationship or the opportunity. If you prepare something ahead of time, make absolutely sure that it's relevant to what you and the prospect are discussing.

Suppose that your customer says to you, "How much is this project going to cost me?" You respond by saying, "The price for this project is $7,500 . . . and 5 cents." At that point, if you've built up any kind of rapport with the prospect, the person is going to laugh and then say something like, "What's the nickel for?" You then respond, "It's just in case you start nickel-and-diming me." And by the way, this is an excellent way to lay the groundwork for the negotiation discussions that are likely to accompany your presentation! Both you and the customer know that there's going to be a point of stress after the topic of price comes up. You both know that you're each going to be trying to get the best terms. If you acknowledge—in a slightly comical way—that you know this will happen, then you will remove a lot of the stress and create an emotional environment that delivers an outcome that's satisfactory to both sides.

As important as humor is to the presentation and to your negotiation discussions, it's just as important to remember that you are there to solve problems and close deals—not to be a stand-up comedian.

You must assess your audience properly if you want your humor to serve your sales process. There are some people who will instantly respond well to joking and others for whom any form of humor will fall flat. Your job is to figure out which kind of person you're dealing with in a given situation, and then figure out what will improve the dialogue with that person. Very often it will be humor. But sometimes it won't. If you try to rely on humor at the wrong moment with the wrong person, you can kill the deal.

Skill #5: Giving Them Options

Of course, it's not just the words and ideas you use that count in your demonstration; it's also the structure in which you present your words and ideas that dictates how your customer will react and respond to your offer.

Many salespeople only give their customers two options at the conclusion of a presentation: yes or no. This is a huge strategic mistake. By focusing on only those two options, we program the customer's mind to address this question: "Am I going to do business with this person or not?" That's the internal question that a yes-or-no option establishes for your audience.

Let's examine the worst-case scenario, which is something leaders always have to consider. Suppose that you didn't create a strong enough value proposition to overcome the perceived risk of working with you. What kind of response are you going to get when you present a yes-or-no, up-or-down, with-me-or-against-me option? You're either going to get a "No," or you're going to get a "Let us think about it" answer. And you know what? You're going to deserve those answers! Why? Because you knew what the worst-case scenario was, and you did nothing to plan for it!

Now let me ask you this: What would happen if you gave your audience three alternatives to consider, and "No, thanks" was not one of them? For instance, suppose you gave your listeners these three options:

Option A: A low-end option that is going to meet their basic needs, even though you know they probably want a little bit more.

Option B: This choice is right on target; it's a solution that looks like it will meet their needs as closely and compellingly as possible. This is the one you would pick if you could point the prospect toward only one possible course of action. As a leader, of course, you are not limited to one course of action, so you can also offer . . .

Option C: This option adds a few more bells and whistles because you think it will give them a high-end result that they hadn't considered.

In other words, instead of asking any variation on "Do we have a deal?" or "When do we get started?" (both of which are versions on the "yes-or-no" question), you ask, "Which looks like the best fit to you—A, B, or C?"

Presenting your customers with three opportunities—instead of two—changes their thinking pattern. Now, instead of processing the question "Am I going to work with this person?" your prospect is asking himself this: "How do I want to work with this person?" You can have a much better conversation once the prospect starts discussing options with you or even proposing new options you hadn't yet imagined. When this happens, you have initiated a true collaboration effort; you are no longer trying to sell the person anything. Once the prospect is fully engaged in figuring out how to work with you, your chances of attaining and closing a lucrative deal skyrocket.

Skill #6: Supporting the Message with the Medium (Not Vice Versa)

In theory, there's nothing wrong with presentation bells and whistles. However, it's imperative to remember that it's not the bells and whistles that are going to carry the day, but rather the leader's ability to land the message.

For better or worse, we live in an era when presentation software like PowerPoint has become an accepted tool for creating, delivering, and receiving professional analyses and recommendations. That's okay, and technology like this can definitely be a powerful resource for your presentation. At the same time, however, you need to make sure that the slide deck you are showing off supports your purpose and does not become the purpose of your meeting.

> **The Leader's Advantage**
>
> The PowerPoint deck is not the presentation. You are the presentation.

With that critical point in mind, consider the following three "Dos and Don'ts" for an effective presentation that incorporates software like PowerPoint.

- *Don't overload the screen with words.* Most people put too many facts and figures on a single slide, and that's not what PowerPoint is for. It's a tool for expressing your presentation's key points and nothing more. If necessary, pass out a handout that has your supporting information after your main presentation is over. When it comes to the number of words that show up on a PowerPoint slide—less is definitely more! Keep any given PowerPoint slide to as few words as possible. If you don't, everybody will be spending their time trying to read the slide instead of looking at you. You need to speak about the additional details that aren't shown on the slide, rather than having the slide do the talking for you.

(The same thing goes for handouts, of course. If you pass
them out while you're still mid-message, you'll lose everyone
in the room because they'll be leafing through the handout.)
- *Use pictures and photographs.* Images wake up your message and
  win your audience's interest and attention. Again, PowerPoint
  was designed to be used with text, art, and photographs. If all
  you're doing is throwing text at people, you'll lose them.
- *Don't read the slide show verbatim.* Your audience doesn't need
  you for that! Use the slide show to spark what you want to
  say next. Then go into detail—detail that doesn't show up on
  the slide. Make sure you land the message with your audience
  before your proceed to the next point.

The whole idea, of course, is to present the outcomes that support
your vision in a vivid way, get the issues on the table, and then get
some feedback. If you have to talk briefly about features as part of
that process, that's fine, but keep in mind that your ultimate goal
job is to uncover and answer all possible questions about what you're
envisioning doing with this prospect.

Although I'm sharing these points with you as they relate to
PowerPoint, the underlying concept here is to use any and all presentation tools—virtual meeting software, videoconference software,
whatever—in support of the same basic goals: present your vision,
get the issues and questions out in the open, and establish a dialogue.
The issue that matters most is your ability to land your point, not
your ability to master PowerPoint design or flashy sounds, graphics,
and video feeds. Yes, image is important, and all of these tools can
be great to the extent that they support your ability to connect with
people. At the end of the day, all that matters is whether or not you
connect with your audience. If there's something wrong with your
computer system and you can't access your PowerPoint, can you still
engage the audience and have the discussion you want to have? If the

answer is "no," then you're relying too heavily on technology and not enough on your own people skills.

If I had to give you one and only one piece of advice about multimedia, it would be this: Keep it simple. The more complex you make the presentation—and the more variables you introduce—the harder it will be to for you to manage your audience. And like a great orchestra conductor, you must be in complete control of the performance. If you are not, then your performance won't be well received.

The Leader's Advantage

If there are handouts that accompany your presentation, I recommend that you hold off handing those out until the end of your talk. The exception is a meeting where everyone knows ahead of time that you will be reviewing your contract. Hand that out at the *beginning* of the meeting, and make sure everyone is (literally and figuratively) on the same page with you as you discuss the various elements of the formal working agreement.

A final thought on supplements or additions to the in-person presentation: In most cases, you shouldn't fax or overnight the presentation to the audience ahead of time because that removes your control of the situation. Since the purpose is to present and supervise the situation while you're in front of the group—by assessing people's reactions, engaging them in dialogue, and responding appropriately—sending materials ahead of time won't do you much good. You can't possibly gauge someone's response over the phone, via fax, through e-mail, or as they open an overnight package. You need to be present to hear and see their reactions, make any necessary changes, and close the deal. By the same token, you don't want to send your presentation ahead of your planned visit. You can't land the message with the group if they have prejudged your message, or are four steps ahead of you.[1]

I realize, of course, that it may not be possible for you to be physically present at each and every presentation you make. Some of the salespeople I work with close hundreds of deals every year. If the business is really important to you, however, or if it represents a sizeable chunk of your income, you should definitely find a way to be there.

The Leader's Advantage

Use the presentation as an opportunity to walk people through your vision of the future and to come to a collaborative decision about how best to implement what you're offering.

Skill #7: Conflict Resolution

A lot of people ask me how to handle objections when they come up during presentations. My answer: Don't think of what you're doing as handling objections. Think of what you're doing as conflict resolution. That's what it really is!

It is not your job to pass judgment on the pushback itself or the reasons behind a conflict that's arisen during your presentation. The

---

[1]The only exception to this rule, in my experience, comes when you are dealing with a group of "A-list" leaders, such as a board of directors or a group of investors, who request a look at your proposal ahead of time so that they can make their discussions with you more productive during a narrow face-to-face time window, such as a board meeting. Of course, if such a group of (fellow) leaders makes this request, you should honor it.

conflict is there for one of two reasons: either the person is using the conflict as a ploy to negotiate better terms, or there really is an issue that you need to resolve. You probably won't know exactly which situation you're looking at when the protests first surface. The only way to find out for sure is to validate the complaints that you're hearing.

Notice that I said "validate"—not necessarily agree with or swear under oath that the person's assessment of your company's problems and the perceived flaws of your offering are accurate. Watch what you say, and remember that litigation is a big part of today's business environment. Validate the pushback by following these three basic steps.

First, *acknowledge* that the person has an issue, without trying to dismiss or minimize it. Simply accept that the person has had this reaction, and let him express it in his own words without challenging or interrupting. Accept that there's a problem and that it's worth talking about.

Second, *empathize.* I can't stress the point enough: This does not mean taking sides on the question of who's right or wrong. Empathizing simply requires you to share in the objector's emotional experience by attempting to see things from his perspective. You're basically identifying the emotion connected with the situation, not the specific events that are under discussion, and expressing support for the person who's experiencing these feelings. Be careful! Responding *to* an emotion is very different than responding *with* emotion. Stay objective and impartial. It's quite possible that the other side is attempting to get you to respond emotionally; this is a classic negotiating ploy. Your job is to remove the sentiment by using dialogue to elevate the conversation to a level where it can reach a point of resolution for both sides.

Third, *use dialogue to change the conversation.* Don't focus on what went wrong or why; that's a negative conversation that's not going to solve anything. Start talking about how you can work together to find a solution. Launch a discussion that focuses on the future and on solutions. That's more motivating—and more productive—than playing games about what did or didn't happen in the past or should have happened. Have a collaborative dialogue about the best way to move forward. This is the stage where it should become clear to you whether you're dealing with a negotiating ploy or a more deeply held concern. But in the vast majority of cases you can't get those signals without first acknowledging the issue raised and empathizing with the person who raised it!

If you plan to deliver the kind of presentation a sales leader delivers, and get the kinds of commitments a leader gets, you must follow this three-step process: acknowledge, empathize, and use dialogue to move toward a collaborative discussion about what to do next.

What's the alternative? A presentation that self-destructs! If you don't acknowledge the validity of what people are saying, they're going to tune you out. Once they decide that you've chosen not to listen to them, they won't bother to listen to your solution. If that's what has happened, then no matter what you come back with—even if it's the best possible solution—your audience simply won't buy into it.

On the other hand, if you choose to keep connecting, validating, and listening, then amazing things are possible—even during situations in which the pushback initially seemed intense. Some of my best deals came about after I followed the steps I've laid out for you here and engineered a significant conflict resolution. Remember the story of the client who purchased all those electronic time stamps that had gone bad? What would have happened if I hadn't acknowledged, empathized, and used dialogue—both within my own company and the customer's company—to find an answer that solved the problem and grew the business?

The Leader's Advantage

Start seeing push-back for what it really is: opportunity. Don't be fearful of issues that come up; they are really horses waiting to be driven across the finish line. The reason that sales leaders get paid the big money is that they use effective communication—specifically all seven of the skills I have shared with you in this chapter—to resolve issues!

Your Chapter Nine Commitment

On the Commitment Sheet that follows, write down what you will do this week to follow through on the following assignments:

1. Identify the three skill areas from the Leadership Communication Profile that you will work on developing this week.
2. Practice delivering three true stories that demonstrate your capacity to provide solutions to your customers. Ideally, the stories should come from your personal experience.

 # COMMITMENT!

(Pronunciation: ko-'mit-mint, Function: noun, Definition: a: an agreement or pledge to do something in the future; b: something pledged c: the state or an instance of being obligated or emotionally impelled, a commitment to a cause)

_____

_____

_____

_____

_____

_____

_____

_____

_____

_____

_____

_____

_____

_____

_____

_____

_____

_____

For more of these sample sheets go to http://www.leadsellorgetoutoftheway.com.

Figure 9.3   Commitment Sheet

10

Holding Yourself Accountable

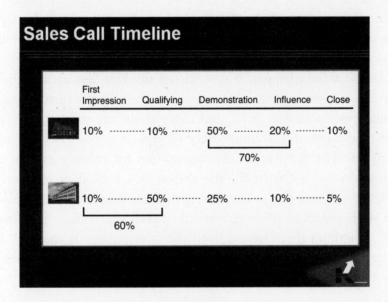

Figure 10.1

The final phase of the sales cycle is the close. There are a lot of effective closing strategies you can use. Some of them are as simple as asking "How do we get started?" Others are as complex as the classic Ben Franklin close, in which you sit down with the prospect and compile two lists: a list of reasons to buy and a list of reasons not to buy, which you then evaluate together. I've got nothing against closing techniques, although some are definitely more effective than others.

What I want you to get from this chapter, however, is not a list of fancy moves you can put on the prospect at the end of the sales process. Rather, I want you to discover how to build accountability into the process at *every* stage, from both sides. If you do that, there's a decent chance of the prospect actually turning to you and saying, "How do we get started?" And that's the outcome that everybody wants.

Unfortunately, not even sales leaders can count on that result all the time. If you're a professional salesperson, you must—by definition—be prepared to ask for the business. However, I think you can make that process easier by embracing this idea of accountability, which is the last of our key sales leadership traits.

What would happen if you started thinking less about how to identify the magic words that you can say to instantly turn a hesitant contact into a customer ... and more about the various ways you can model personal accountability *throughout the sales cycle* for your prospect? That way, when the time comes for either person to say, "How do we get started?" the answer is a natural progression of events that arises out of everything that has happened previously in the relationship. In this scenario—the leader's scenario—the close is not something that's ironed onto the sales process at the end, but rather it is the genuine result of a connection you've built with an ally that is based on your collective vision.

The Big Misconception

I talk to a lot of different companies about how they can improve sales effectiveness, and I've noticed something over the years. I suspect a lot of other sales professionals have noticed the same thing. Our prospects, and even some of our clients, tend to operate under a major misconception, one that is apparent when they come to us and say, "Our people need help with their closing skills. Come on in, and give a program that will show them how to close more deals."

That's a little bit like going to the doctor and saying, "Listen, I've got this cough, and we both know that you could just give me a pill to make it go away. I'm in a hurry, so could you just write me out a prescription right now without putting that stick down my throat?"

First of all, the cough is a symptom—it's not the problem itself. Second of all, you don't really know what's causing the cough; so until the doctor reaches a diagnosis, neither you nor the doctor is in a position to decide on any kind of medication. Whatever is making you sick has already invaded your system well before the moment you started coughing, and it's in everyone's best interest to figure out what that something is.

By the same token, if you've got a lot of salespeople who are delivering deals that typically collapse at the last moment, the problem is not sub-par closing skills.

The Leader's Advantage

The fact that deals aren't closing is a symptom of a poor sales process, not the cause.

The job at hand is to fix the cause, which could be any one of a dozen factors or combination of factors that might be going wrong before the person actually attempts to ask for the order.

At the same time, there is a paradox to consider here. If you're consistently having problems landing the deal, then yes, there probably is something wrong with your closing skills. Now, that may sound like a contradiction with what you just read, but it really isn't.

If you wish to sell like a leader, you must develop closing skills that kick in at the beginning of the process, not the end. By now, I hope you are aware that closing the deal must arise as a natural progression that draws on the work you've done up to that point with the buying organization. Well, if there is no natural progression of commitments whereby you move the relationship towards escalating accountability, agreement, commitments, and trust, then there is definitely not going to be any close when you ask for the business!

Believe it! There are a whole lot of little agreement along the way to the big commitment that you and I refer to as closing the deal, and those commitments should be getting increasingly significant as you near the moment when it makes sense to ask for the business. You have to get commitments in return along the way. If you're always giving them and never getting any in return, then you're not selling as a leader sells!

Let's say that you're at the very beginning of the selling cycle, and you call your contact to request a meeting at a certain date and time. How good a job did you do of asking for and receiving that commitment before making a parallel commitment of your own (for instance, promising to send or e-mail information)? Or, let's say that you're well along in the sales cycle, and the prospect asks you to do some kind of heavy-duty research and analysis that will help him to "get a clearer picture of where things stand." Do you simply start in on the work? Or do you ask what's going to happen if you actually do what the prospect is asking you to do?

These are both examples of modest closes, minor requests for some accountability from the prospect's side in exchange for a comparable piece of accountability from you. There are a lot of smaller closes that must precede the big close that we want to secure. There must be a natural progression of commitments from both sides. If the only time you try to get a commitment of any kind is when you want the business, then you're going to have big problems!

The Leader's Advantage

Closing skills don't only come into play at the end of the cycle; in fact, the close began taking place the moment you said "hello" to this person. The final sale is nothing more than the sum total of the progression of commitments you and the prospect have made along the way.

Leaders Are Accountable to Themselves First

True sales leaders set extremely high standards for themselves, far higher than any standards that anyone else could possibly set for them. They then do whatever it takes to meet those standards. Leaders know that they alone are accountable for their own performance, day in and day out.

The tendency for a salesperson to hold himself accountable is one of the easiest ways to distinguish sales leaders from sales followers. Sales followers are quick to find fault, assign blame, or take other people to task for problems in their world. Sales leaders, on the other hand, know that they are personally responsible for their response to each and every experience in their life and commitment they have made. If something goes wrong, they look to themselves first and ask, "What could I have done differently to deliver a different result?"

If you ever hear a salesperson blame management, or the economy, or a difficult prospect, or anything or anyone else for losing a deal that he should have won, you may rest assured that you are listening to a sales follower, not a sales leader. Sales leaders adopt an attitude of personal responsibility for all their outcomes. Attitude, not events, is what determines success.

"You're Fired!"

Accountability, in fact, starts with attitude. When I began my career as a professional speaker and consultant back in 1988, I took an office in a complex of executive suites. My next-door neighbor was a company that operated a satellite office with a single salesperson. Every morning, I would come in and talk to this salesperson over coffee in his office. To this day, I can't forget those conversations, though I wish I could. They were some of the most depressing conversations I've ever had.

Every morning, without fail, this salesperson would complain about how bad business was, how little notice his company gave him before changing policies, how disloyal his customers were, and so on. It really got the day off to a bad start. I tried to tell him that I wanted to talk about more upbeat subjects, but it didn't make any difference. He kept right on complaining, morning after morning. Finally, I had to send him the message: "You're fired." I didn't literally say those words, but my actions did when I started drinking my morning coffee elsewhere.

I had to make this change because his outlook was starting to affect my business. Looking back, I know I would make the same choice again in a heartbeat. Leaders do not spend more time than is absolutely necessary with people who see the world as a trap. When they hear that kind of talk consistently, they change team members—and acquaintances—fast. Make sure you follow the same policy and apply it to anyone in your circle: colleagues, friends, relatives, whoever.

Hold yourself accountable for creating an environment that will allow you to succeed.

At the end of each of this book's main chapters, you were asked to make specific commitments related to each of the sales leadership traits addressed here. It is now time for you to do a reality check:

The Leader's Wisdom

"I am responsible. Although I may not be able to prevent the worst from happening, I am responsible for my attitude toward the inevitable misfortunes that darken life. Bad things do happen; how I respond to them defines my character and the quality of my life. I can choose to sit in perpetual sadness, immobilized by the gravity of my loss, or I can choose to rise from the pain and treasure the most precious gift I have—life itself."
—Walter Anderson

How good a job would you say you have done when it comes to clarifying and following through on *all* the commitments you have made in the past? What number would you give yourself on a scale of one to 10? Write your answer on a separate piece of paper.

Unless you wrote down a 10 (and if you did, you should be writing this book instead of me), I have a question for you: What are you going to do differently to improve upon that number?

If you resisted writing down a number at all or if your answer is that someone or something else kept you from following through, then you may need to review this chapter a couple of times.

The Leader's Advantage

Effective leaders lead their lives with this mantra: "The buck stops here."

In the final analysis, *you* are the one who must follow through on and implement the important lessons you learn in life. Of course, that includes the commitments you made to yourself earlier in this book. That means you are responsible for the five steps of personal accountability:

- accepting personal responsibility for changing your behaviors;
- taking action to implement the new behaviors and commitments you made in Chapters 3 through 8;
- monitoring the results closely;
- noticing what's working and what's not; and
- changing course as necessary so that you're creating more momentum toward the leadership selling model every day.

Remember, your ultimate accountability is to yourself. People who make personal responsibility a habit in their lives are inevitably accountable to themselves first. If you make promises to yourself and don't keep them, then how can you expect to keep your promises to others? How can you expect your allies to follow through on their commitments to you?

Your success depends not so much on what you have read in this book, but rather on what you do as a result of reading this book.

Getting Off the Launching Pad

I remember an experience I had a few years back with a client who wanted me to help him with personal coaching, so that he could approach his business with a new perspective and take it to a more profitable level. We sat down together and looked at his situation, and we drew up an entirely new business plan for his company. We then set up some actionable steps for him to carry out and agreed to meet weekly so that we could work together as he implemented the plan.

The problem was that he didn't implement the plan. We met for three straight weeks, and each week he had taken absolutely no action to employ the blueprint we'd spent all that time putting together!

I said to him, "I have to be honest. I'm frustrated here, because obviously this is something you are not really committed to. Maybe I'm not connecting with you in the way that I should be, but I'm trying, and at the end of the day it's just a waste of time for you and for me to keep meeting every week. I really can't help you if you're not really motivated to make this thing happen."

His wife, who was a schoolteacher, happened to be in the room, and she had a big problem with what I had just said to her husband. She told me, "If I said that to my students, their parents would be all over me. You're a teacher. You've got a responsibility for the outcome here."

I replied, "I have to disagree. My job is to create an environment that brings the best out of my clients, but in the end, nothing will happen if the client himself does not the have desire to do whatever it takes to achieve the results."

And I truly believe this. If the rocket is going to get off the launching pad, someone has to hit "launch," and when it comes right down to it, no teacher or mentor can hit "launch" for you. You have to launch yourself.

The difference between successful people and those who are complaining about not being successful is this: The successful people are consistently taking action on the things that need to be done, even if they don't like doing them. The unsuccessful people aren't taking any action at all.

So, now that you've had a chance to read this book, it all comes down to you. What are you going to do to take action? What are you going to do to implement what you've learned?

Quality of Success Actions

Making a clear plan and then executing it in a way that is consistent with your goal is the kind of accountability I see in sales leaders, and this is the first thing I try to help salespeople do when the time comes to implement the principles I've shared with you in this book. When I talk about business planning for sales executives, I always start with the end in sight. I begin by focusing on the main goal that they're working toward and then identify the key milestones, activities, or actions that have to happen for my clients to reach that results.

Let's say that you want to make $1.2 million in sales in a year. That means that you have to generate $100,000 in revenues per month or perhaps a $300,000 deal every quarter. Once you have identified these crucial milestones, you can continue working your way back and identifying the fundamental activities that are going to be necessary for you to achieve your results. I call these activities your Quality of Success Actions. These are the actions for which you are going to hold yourself personally accountable for executing on a daily basis.

I'd like to share with you how I chose the name Quality of Success Actions. You may have read a lot about the credit that New York Mayor Rudy Giuliani received for lowering crime rates in New York City during his time in office. In 1994, when crime was a key issue in New York politics, Giuliani successfully implemented the ideas that were already in development within the New York City Police Department. Known as the ComStat System, this new program tracked crimes that were taking place in the city with a precision and thoroughness that had been previously considered impossible. The reason that the ComStat System was so groundbreaking—for Giuliani and every other New York mayor who followed him—was that it enabled people to use complex statistical tools to increase the flow of meaningful information about crimes between precinct commanders.

Twice a week, the precinct commanders would have to come to police headquarters to discuss the crime trends in their precincts. During those meetings, the commanders were held accountable for the activity that was taking place in their neighborhoods. The commander had no excuse for being unaware of what was happening in his or her precinct and no excuse for not having a plan in place to address the most pressing problem. The police commissioner, mayor, and other city executives would evaluate the plan to determine whether there were any holes in it. ComStat made this discussion possible, because precinct commanders now had a clearer picture than ever before about what was actually taking place in their world.

In addition to tracking the serious crimes such as rapes, murder, and burglary, the ComStat system also allowed the precinct commanders to identify certain critical activities that were most likely to produce a high-crime environment in the city, such as motorists being accosted at red lights with offers to clean their windshields and the oldest trade known to mankind—prostitution. Even though they weren't classified as major crimes, both of these activities had a strong statistical correlation with elevated crime rates in the city, and there were two substantial reasons for this. First, these activities made a statement about what kind of environment people were living in, and second, the people who engaged in them were likely to move on to other crimes.

Here's the point. Officials in New York City called these activities *quality of life* crimes; if the police were able to crack down on these offenders and get them off the streets, they'd be able to have the maximum positive impact on the city's quality of life. Basically, the ComStat System enabled the New York City Police Department to make a quantum leap in terms of law enforcement efficiency by helping it to focus on the right activities.

What does any of that have to do with you? Everything! You can use the same process that the NYPD used to reduce crime in the city to build up your sales. You'll start with the most important resource: accurate and timely intelligence. You first identify your goals and milestones and then track how you're actually doing against those milestones on a weekly and monthly basis. You'll ask yourself: "What actions will determine the Quality of Success in my life?"

The Leader's Advantage

One big difference between sales leaders and followers is that leaders constantly hold themselves accountable for the connection between their daily activities and their own progress toward a long-term goal.

Go back to our example of the $1.2 million quota for the year. Let's suppose you break it down to $100,000 a month and that you have a sales cycle that makes that target realistic. When do you start measuring whether you are behind quota? For instance, do you start measuring that at the end of the first half of the year? If you do, you have to have $600,000 in business in hand at the point when you *start* measuring! Wouldn't you want to give yourself more time to correct your daily strategy if you found a problem? There's a lot that could go wrong in those first six months, and there might be quite a bit of ground to make up if you were initially off target. If you measured on a weekly or monthly basis, however, you'd leave a lot more options open if you had to make up some ground. The NYPD measured their results on a weekly basis, and held intense, plan-focused evaluations on exactly what they had to do about those results twice a week. Are you willing to hold yourself to the same standard? And if you aren't, why not?

The Leader's Advantage

What really matters is (a) what you measure and (b) how often you measure it.

Once you identify the critical benchmarks, you want to take your basis of calculation and connect it to the shortest time element possible. Why? Because the sooner you find out whether or not your actions are strong enough to support your purpose, the more time you will have to make changes to your plan. If there are problems, you want to be able to deploy additional resources so you can compensate for any shortfall and ensure that you achieve your desired sales goal at the end of the year (if you're working against an annual goal).

One side comment here for senior executives, CEOs, and business owners: Some companies are highly seasonal in nature. Yet I see management at many of those companies giving salespeople the same quota each month, whether or not that month is part of their big selling season. Don't make this mistake; adjust your monthly numbers to correlate with your industry's seasonal trends. There's nothing less motivating for a salesperson than having to hit an unrealistic sales target in a month when it's all but impossible to do so.

Of course, we are not *just* talking about benchmarks like $1.2 million for the year means $100,000 per month. You are also going to have to identify your Quality of Success Actions. Just as the New York City Police Department identified certain activities that had the highest possible chance of improving the quality of life in the city, you can identify certain activities that have the highest possible chance of improving the quality of your success.

Quality of Success Actions differ from one salesperson to the next and from one sales position to the next. Every salesperson gravitates to the style of selling that suits him or her best, and every sales position demands that the salesperson adopt a certain set of actions. But there are definitely actions that you can take that will dramatically affect the quality of your success—that is, the speed and efficiency with which you move toward your benchmarks. For you, a Quality of Success Action might mean making X number of new calls to new prospects per week. Or it might entail setting up a direct mail campaign or an e-newsletter and following through on all the queries that result. Or it might involve going to events where you know your prospects are going to congregate—a trade show, for instance—once a quarter.

You need to identify the Quality of Success Actions that will have the biggest impact in your world. You need to establish and execute a plan that allows you to use those actions on a consistent basis to turn your benchmarks into realities—one that gets you where you want to go.

Whenever I am called in by a CEO or vice president of sales to evaluate a sales team, I immediately look for two things: the Quality of Success Actions that are currently delivering measurable progress toward monthly benchmarks and the actual year-to-date progress against those benchmarks for each team member and the group as a whole. Once I have that information I can tell—with complete accuracy—who is going to achieve their goal and who is not. Just as the ComStat System gave the precinct commanders of the New York City Police Department the information they needed to develop the right plan, those two measures give me the information I need to figure out who needs help.

Here is a sample list of Quality of Success Actions that may or may not be relevant to your industry. Whether or not they apply to your business, you can use them to develop your own list of the actual steps you have to take on a consistent basis to meet your personal sales benchmarks.

Sample Quality of Success Actions

(Warning: These are different for every salesperson; use this list as a model only. "X" is the number that makes sense in your environment, based on your selling cycle and your individual income targets)

- Send a monthly e-zine out to existing clients and prospects with tips on industry trends and new product/service enhancements

- Call X existing clients each morning before making first sales call to investigate new business opportunities
- Call X new qualified prospects each morning before first sales appointment
- Identify X new qualified business opportunities each week
- Communicate with all allies (advocates, partners, associates, colleagues, existing customers) on a regular basis
- Attend X major tradeshows each year
- Attend local monthly networking events, and follow-up next day on leads
- Get X qualified referrals per week
- Make X final presentations each week

The Sales Process

Of course, all of these Quality of Success Activities connect to a broader sequence of events: your sales process. Most salespeople don't connect the daily, weekly, or monthly actions that will actually deliver the result they're after to the sales process as a whole. To help you connect the dots, I've identified what I call a Sales Success Activity Plan. It's a completed plan that uses an annual target of $500,000, and works backward to identify the necessary benchmarks in all the key categories of the sales process.

Starting with the goal first, this plan calls for $500,000 in revenues for the year with an average sale of $5,000. That means that 100 deals are needed for the year. Let's suppose the salesperson has a 60 percent closing ratio at the presentation/demonstration phase (which means 60 percent of all presentations/demonstrations lead to a sale). To figure out how many presentations you need at that rate to get 100 deals,

Sample Sales Success
Activity Plan

Contacts	**(10%) 20,900**
Prospects	**(20%) 2090**
Needs Assessment	**(40%) 418**
Presentation/Demonstration	**(60%) 167**
Close	**($5,000 per) 100**
Gross Yearly Income or Sales	**$500,000**

Bottom # Divided by %

Figure 10.2

you simply divide 100 by 60 percent. Follow the same procedure for each step of the selling cycle listed on the plan. As you will see once you've done all the math, you will need to have 20,900 contacts or touches with your market that year if you want to reach your goal of 100 deals.

Don't get alarmed; it's actually not that hard to do. For example, I have an e-zine list that includes several thousand people. If your list has 4,000 people on it and you just sent out an e-zine every month, then you'll contact 4,000 potential customers a month. (These should obviously be quality contacts, and you will want to avoid over-mailing to your list.) The point is that sending out that e-zine once a month is one of my Quality of Success Actions. I know what mine are; do you know what yours are?

The whole point of this exercise is to identify the key steps in your sales cycle, and then identify the level of activity you will need to take in order to reach your goal. You need to start figuring out your closing ratios at the end of each step of the process. Many salespeople have no clue what those numbers are. If you don't know your own statistics, how will you know what you have to do to succeed? How will you know what you are accountable to yourself for?

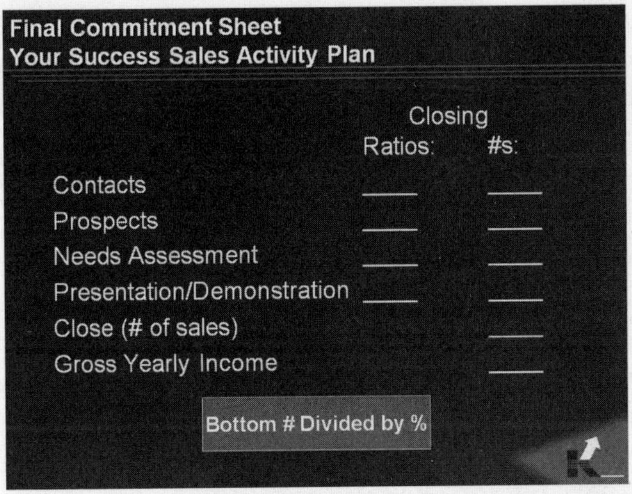

Final Commitment Sheet
Your Success Sales Activity Plan

	Closing Ratios:	#s:
Contacts	____	____
Prospects	____	____
Needs Assessment	____	____
Presentation/Demonstration	____	____
Close (# of sales)		____
Gross Yearly Income		____

Bottom # Divided by %

Figure 10.3

Your Chapter Ten Commitment

Figure 10.3 contains a blank commitment form for you to use to develop your own plan. Please don't forget to customize the steps for your sales cycle; if you incorporate more than seven milestones, the plan is too complex.

And now—before I conclude this important chapter—I want to share some advice on how to use the form above. *Always shoot for more than what you want; follow the 25 Percent Rule.*

This is the sales equivalent of a safety tip. It protects you against unexpected downturns in the market. I am always shooting for results that are at least 25 percent above my original goal. (Often, I'm shooting even higher.) Because my current actions are aimed at a higher level, I have a much better chance of reaching my original goal, and I won't be devastated if I happen to hit a bump in the road.

The story of Control Data Corporation (CDC) illustrates the importance of this point. In the mid-1980s, CDC was one of the biggest companies in the country, and even appeared on the *Fortune 100* list. (The problems that they subsequently faced, however, forced them out of the top 100—and eventually out of the top 500.) But at this point in time, CDC was still a prestigious member of the Fortune 100 and owned the largest and most successful disk drive manufacturing business in the country. I worked for a small division of that business unit whose job it was to take the disk and tape drives manufactured by CDC, package them as standalone units, and sell them to corporations. My territory was the Northeast United States, and most of my business came from the Tri-State area: New York, New Jersey, and Connecticut.

Even though it was a major player in the computer industry, CDC was in trouble. It was starting to lose market share at an alarming rate. Demand for its big mainframe computers was dropping through the floor, thanks to the development of minicomputers and personal computers.

There was another problem: My competitors purchased the same drives I was selling from my parent company on an OEM (original equipment manufacturer) basis at cheaper prices than I could get internally! How could this be? As a division of CDC, we had to charge an extra 15 percent to cover our contribution to support corporate overhead. By the time we came to market, our prices were much higher than my competition's—even after our discounts. And the competition was selling the product manufactured by *my* company!

Clearly, my division was in a bad situation. We realized that if we continued to sell in the same way that we had been, we were not going to achieve our goals. So we decided to sell our disk drives to resellers in hopes of increasing the volume of units sold. Because our prices were much higher than the competition's, my new job was to go out and find a reseller who needed me as much as I needed them—and in a hurry.

Every Sunday, I had seen ads in the newspaper for a computer integrator in Princeton called Clancy Paul. I picked up the phone and got in touch with the company president Glen Paul, who had just graduated from Princeton University. His plan was to build a business by being the best systems integrator in the Princeton area that catered to Fortune 500 companies.

I began my discussion with Glen by asking an issues-based question: What was his biggest challenge? He said, "My biggest challenge is money and credibility. I want to be the best systems integrator for the top corporations located down here in Princeton, and I can't do it if I don't have credibility with them. And I only have six months to develop this business before the money runs out."

I told Glen that CDC was number 84 on the Fortune 100 list (which was the case, at that point) and that if he signed with us, I would publish a press release saying that we had just signed on to a strategic relationship with Clancy Paul. This was music to his ears. Even though my products were priced much higher than the competition's, he decided to take the risk of spending the extra money because he needed the credibility of being associated with a key player in his desired market.

Remember the 25 Percent Rule? It came into play here. Business had been really bad for us at this time—Fortune 100 listing or no Fortune 100 listing. In an attempt to keep us motivated, CDC had lowered our quotas from $1.2 million to $800,000—a massive reduction of expectations. But I hadn't lowered my personal expectations. Failure was not an option for me. The individual goal I set for myself—for which I held myself accountable that year—was not $800,000. In fact, it wasn't even $1.2 million; it was $1.5 million. And it was only because I held myself responsible for that aggressive (some might say absurd) goal in a down market that I was motivated enough to keep looking for the needle in the haystack. I eventually found that needle: It was called Clancy Paul.

Against all odds, I was one of only two sales executives who came in on plan at CDC that year. I actually beat the $1.2 million quota!

Here's a final thought about accountability: Your results are only going to be as strong as the guiding purpose for which you are willing to hold yourself accountable—and on which you are going to take consistent action—in your life.

The guiding purpose that I'm talking about will always inspire you to take responsibility for the quality of your actions. It will sustain you and energize you during the inevitable setbacks and downturns you will face, and it will always point you toward the future, growth, constructive change, and new things you can do to both move forward in your own life and help others move forward. True leaders are driven by this kind of high purpose, one that draws people to them and summons everyone—including the leader—to a new and higher level of achievement. What's the alternative? Doing what you've always done.

Ultimately, your guiding purpose is not about you. It is about the positive impacts you are driven to make in other people's lives and businesses. There is only one reason that someone will buy from you: because he believes that doing so will help him to reach an important destination in life. Bring people to that destination. Make getting people where they want to go your guiding purpose, and be passionate about fulfilling that purpose. After all, as so many leaders have shown by example, there can be no true accountability without passion and purpose.

Epilogue

In the early 1980s, I was an emergency medical technician (EMT) serving on the Volunteer Ambulance Corps in Fair Lawn, NJ. Getting my EMT certification was a challenging task that involved more than 120 hours of classroom and field study, ending with both a written and field test. I took the field test in a wide-open gym where my case was a person with a severe back injury lying on the ground. We had a huge amount of room in which to be evaluated on the ABC's of first aid: maintain open Airways, make sure the patient is Breathing, and do whatever it takes to ensure proper Circulation of blood. If you moved the patient in any way that could have impeded the ABCs, you immediately failed the test.

Now, pretend the scene of the accident involved an old Volkswagen Beetle—a very small two-door car—wrapped around a telephone pole. The patient is crushed between the dashboard and seat with the steering wheel in between. Gone is all that extra room to move around and work on the patient that I had during the test in the gym. Obviously, I could make some improvisations when moving the patient in such a difficult situation. However, because of the strict training that my fellow EMTs and I endured, the concept of compromising the ABCs was always in the forefront of our minds and part of every decision we made. Regardless of whatever else we had to do, we could not under any circumstance inhibit the patient's ABCs; otherwise, there would be no patient left to move.

In this book, you have been given all the tools you need to increase your sphere of influence, dramatically grow your sales, and hone your leadership skills. Just as in the world of first aid, there are ABCs—certain fundamental actions—that can *never* be compromised in order to get the deal. For instance, you must gain the time and attention of anyone you are looking to influence. To do that, you must effectively communicate the positive outcomes that they can expect as a result of working with you and buying from you.

You then must ask the right questions to uncover and build your Delta of Opportunity. This involves finding out where the customer is trying to go, developing a clearer picture of how you can help them get there, and identify the consequences of actions. Following that, you must persuasively communicate the solutions you have pinpointed and close the deal.

Whatever you do, your actions should always center on the customer. I have given you the agenda; now it is time for you to customize this process appropriately for each situation that you encounter. Some sales can be made on one call, while others can take weeks, months, or even years to close, depending on the size and complexity of the deal. No matter how complicated or simple the deal is, the same process and tools outlined in this book will work for you. The only difference is how they are employed and to what extent.

Keep your focus on the customer and you will never go wrong. Help people get the outcomes they are after, you will always be a success.

The bottom line is that you have the ability to increase your sphere of influence and sales just by the way you act toward those you are trying to influence. It's worth repeating: In all of my years of working with clients, I've found that the ones who have achieved the greatest market share, closed the most deals, and increased their profit the most all had one thing in common: They changed the conversations they were having with their customers. They never changed their products or services. We may have branded them differently, but in virtually every case, they kept their products and services in place. They simply altered the way they presented those products and services.

Here's the moral of the story: You're in charge. You have the power to lead your customers through their buying decisions. Your actions will dictate their response and your success.

Finally, Let Me Introduce You to Phil

Have you ever had one of those trips where everything just seemed to go completely wrong—the business trip from Hell? I was going down to Jacksonville, Florida, to speak at a national sales meeting. I took a three-hour flight that ended up lasting 10 hours.

I remember finally pulling up to the Omni Hotel in Jacksonville. As I got out of my rental car, there were only two things I wanted in life: room service and a bed. I opened the door, dragged my body out of the car and simply stood in front of the hotel—if you could even call what I was doing standing. My shoulders were hunched over and drooped, and I was fighting to keep from falling asleep in that very spot. Talk about being a motivational speaker; I was what you might call motivationally impaired at that particular moment.

Out of the corner of my barely opened eye, I caught a glimpse of a bright shining light that turned to be the setting sun bouncing off of a set of perfectly white teeth attached to an extremely tall man in a hotel uniform. This giant began to make his way over to me, his shadow looming larger with each and every step. Emotionally spent and tired, I simply prayed that he would just walk past me. He approached, appeared ready to keep on going, and all of a sudden he came to a complete halt in front of me, smiled, and asked in a booming voice, "Sir, what's your name?"

I looked up into this enormous man's eyes, and with all the strength I could muster, said, "Karr, K-A-R-R." He replied, "*You're*

Mr. Karr?" Doing my best *All in the Family* Archie Bunker impression, I responded, "YES!!!!!!" He said, "You don't understand. I've been waiting to meet you all day long."

All of a sudden, that feeling of motivational impairment miraculously began to disappear. I replied with childlike incredulity, "You *have*?" And the tall man answered with a wink, "Yes sir! When I heard that Mr. Karr was coming in, I said to myself, I've got to meet that fine gentleman."

I wondered: What did the hotel say to this guy? "We've got this important speaker, take care of him!" The giant, whose name turned out to be Phil coming in, saw that my mind was wandering, and he winked at me again. And that's when it came to me: He says this to every guest he meets!

Even after I realized that Phil greeted every guest to the hotel in the same way, I was in awe of him. He had transformed my whole day and instantly improved my emotional state.

I thought to myself "This is just too good to be true." I said, "Phil, this is an incredible story about great customer service. Being a bellhop is such an important position. You represent the first experience a guest has when coming to this hotel. Management must have known that this was the job for you when they hired you."

Phil looked at me and said, "What, are you kidding me? My first job was in housekeeping."

"Housekeeping?" I asked incredulously.

"Yeah," he replied. "Can you imagine me being in a room all day long making beds by myself?"

"Well," I asked, "what happened?"

He told me: "One day I was in this room making beds, and I was having an incredible conversation, and a couple of managers came down the hall. They walked in to see what the ruckus was all about, and they asked me who I was talking to. I replied, 'No one' and they said, 'No one? If you're going to have this kind of conversation with no one, imagine what you could be doing if you had someone to talk to?' So they promoted me, and they made me a bellhop."

After I took in that story, I said, "Phil, you're at the top of your game, aren't you?" And that's when Phil looked at me and winked again—and taught me one of the most valuable lessons I've ever learned.

He said, "Mr. Karr, the truth is, I've had some great days in my life, but I've yet to have the *best* day of my life."

And isn't that what it's all about? Isn't that why we go to meetings and read books like this? To find out the information that we need to take our performance up to the next level week after week, day after day? Isn't *that* what it's all about?

Here is my solemn promise to you: I promise you that if you provide that spontaneous combustion of caring to your customers, if you do whatever it takes to make them feel valued, and if you do whatever it takes to produce their desired results, then you will achieve your desired level of success. Help people get to where they want to be; you will in turn get more than you ever thought was possible. Do this every day and you will be doing what Phil is doing: living a life in which each and every day is truly the best day of your life.

Appendix: Productivity Tools for Sales Leaders

This section contains a list of vendors, professional service providers, and resources that will help salespeople live the life of a sales leader as defined throughout this book. These resources do not represent all possible options in each category. They simply include the resources of which I am aware and, in some cases, resources I have used in my business. When you are considering whether to use a specific type of resource, please feel free to contact them and mention where you heard their name. If for some reason you still feel you need something else that is not listed here, I would suggest that you Google your requests.

CRM's Customer Relationship Manager Software

ACT
http://www.act.com
ACT! helps individuals and small-business owners work more effectively. With ACT! you can easily access a complete,

integrated view of your contact relationships, impress contacts with your follow up, leave no task undone, and make informed decisions to advance your business.

Salesforce.com

http://www.salesforce.com

Easy-to-use Web-based CRM solution for sales, service, marketing, and call center operations that streamlines customer relationship management and boosts customer satisfaction. Organizations can enjoy unparalleled productivity, revenue growth, and business intelligence with Salesforce CRM.

Databases

Hoovers

http://www.hoovers.com/

Offers "company information with detailed business reports and industry profiles." Often has more and better information on individual contacts than competing services. This is a great tool, one that I have used for several years.

Infousa

http://www.infousa.com/

Mailing lists and e-mail lists for businesses of all sizes.

Jigsaw

http://www.jigsaw.com

"Business directory of business contacts and company information." A great prospecting tool. This is a membership-based service, where you can trade names from your list for other salespeople's lists or simply buy names. FYI, I never trade my list, as I believe that is proprietary information and my clients would not appreciate it.

Lead411

http://www.lead411.com

"Provides sales leads, business email lists, company profiles, and lead generation tools."

Salesgenie

www.salesgenie.com

Extremely flexible interface offering profiles of more than 14 million U.S. businesses, including information on individual contacts. Part of InfoUSA.

USADATA

www.usadata.com

Bills itself as "the leading provider of sales leads on demand through on-demand web-based solutions for customer acquisition and customer relationship management." More than 100,000 businesses have secured leads from USAData.

ZoomInfo

www.Zoominfo.com

The pre-eminent business information search engine offering "profiles on more than 45 million people and 4 million companies." Good source of background information on "industries, companies, people, products, services and jobs."

Marketing

Constant Contact

www.constantcontact.com

The premiere no-hassle e-mail marketing service for small- and mid-sized businesses and, of course, individual salespeople. The service "makes it easy to create professional HTML email campaigns with no tech skills," a promise that it actually fulfills. Very little effort translates into a highly polished, professional look. Offers a free 60-day trial. I use this program to distribute my e-zine and automatically manage my mailing list. Highly recommended.

Networking

Ecademy
http://www.ecademy.com
Established in 1998, Ecademy is a business social network with millions of users worldwide.
Ecademy enables business people to connect through online networking, at business networking events and at meetings.

Facebook
http://www.facebook.com
A massively popular social networking website that allows members to join networks based on region, workplace, school, and other parameters. The site has attracted 132 million unique users to date.

MySpace
http://www.MySpace.com
Another extremely popular social networking site estimated to attract over 200,000 new users per day. MySpace provides content in 15 languages and offers more graphic customization to users than Facebook; each site, however, has its passionate adherents. Many users have profiles on both sites.

LinkedIn
http://www.linkedin.com
As of this writing, this is the premier business-oriented networking site. If you don't have a profile here, you should. Currently LinkedIn has a total of 24 million registered users and monthly

traffic of over 3.2 million visitors. Spans over 150 industries, including, in all likelihood, a number that could be buying from you.

Plaxo

http://www.plaxo.com

An online address book and social networking service. Roughly 20 million users.

Twitter

http://www.twitter.com

Twitter has become the service of choice for friends, families, and co-workers eager to communicate and stay connected through the exchange of quick, frequent answers to one simple question: What are you doing now? This short messaging service works over multiple networks and devices, and is an increasingly indispensable business communication tool.

Tripit

http://www.tripit.com

Travel a lot? You should check out this service. It lets you quickly organize all your travel plans—flights, lodging, cars, trains, cruises, whatever—and automatically generate itineraries, complete with weather, maps, restaurants, and much more.

Sales Team Productivity Resource

iLearningGlobal

http://www.ilearningglobal.tv

The iLearningGlobal community is changing the way individuals learn and improve themselves on a daily basis. By becoming a member of iLearningGlobal, you gain access to today's most dynamic speakers and trainers in a way you've never seen them before. iLearningGlobal presents a growing library of these speeches in an amazing high-definition, full-screen video format along with audio programs, e-books, live webcasts, and much more. Personal development and quality business training has never been more important than it is today. iLearning-Global.tv delivers the best to you 24/7! Full Disclosure: I am a member of the iLearningGlobal faculty.

Makana
www.makanasolutions.com
For sales managers. Excellent resource for sales compensation best practices.

Microsoft Office Outlook
http://office.microsoft.com/en-us/outlook/
Popular personal scheduling and organizing software that is part of the Office suite that includes Word, PowerPoint and Excel. Capable of consolidating e-mail and scheduling functions. Many of your prospects live their business lives through this software, so it's probably a language you should be able to speak. According to Microsoft, the software "provides an integrated solution for managing your time and information, connecting across boundaries, and remaining in control of the information that reaches you." All true!

ELance
http://www.elance.com
Great site for finding resources to do web development work, creative work, write sales pitches, admin and technical support, and so on. All you have to do is list your project and people will bid on it. Within hours, you will find someone who has the skills you need at the budget you can afford.

International Virtual Assistants Association

http://www.ivaa.org/

Don't want to pay for full-time help with benefits? Want part timers who are well qualified and can help you in any part of your business? Virtual assistants are a great resource in helping admin your business.

VR+ Software

http://store.handmark.com

You can upload, store, and manage your recordings with VR+ Online Service and popular social networks like MySpace, FaceBook, and Twitter. This software is great; I use it to capture my ideas any time of the day by dictating into my Blackberry, which then uploads it and sends it to me in an e-mail.

Or Contact Us Directly!

Reach out to Karr Associates, Inc. with any questions you may have about anything. We will either help you personally or guide you in the right direction. When it comes to growing your sales, negotiating tough deals, developing leadership within the organization, and helping to create the vision and plan of attack, we can help.

Karr Associates, Inc.

http://www.ronkarr.com

"Specializes in helping organizations and professionals generate remarkable sales and operational results."

Sign up for your free monthly e-zine on *Lead, Sell, or Get Out of the Way* at www.ronkarr.com.

For additional forms referred to in this book, go to http://www. leadsellorgetoutoftheway.com.

Index

Landing the point, 190
Lead, Sell, or Get Out of the Way Accountability Program, 238
Lead, taking the, 199–200
Lead411, 239
Leadership Communication Profile, 179–180
audience and opportunity assessment, 186–194
conflict resolution, 206–208
congruence, 183–186
humor, using, 198–200
message translation, 194–198
options, offering, 200–202
presentation tools, appropriate use of, 202–206
Leadership mix, 9–11
Leadership selling, as a continuous process, 5–6
LeBlanc, Mark, 106
Liability, building alliances and, 92
LinkedIn, 107–108, 241
Listening
building alliances and, 98–99
vs. hearing, 136–137
Lombardi, Vince, 125
"Lone Ranger" selling model, 2
Long-term vision, 50

Makana, 242
Mantle, Mickey, 21–22, 23
Marketing resources, 240
Mattingly, Don, 22–23
McDonalds, 132
Media relations, as an intangible motivator, 164
Meet the Press, 35
Mergers, alliances as an alternative to, 109
Merriam Webster Dictionary, 130
Message translation, 194–198
Microsoft Office Outlook, 243
Modifications: visualization and, 46
Money, as a distraction, 31. *See also* Prices
Monologues, avoiding, xviii, 3, 4
Motivators, value propositions and, 162
emotional, 167–169
intangible, 164–166
tangible, 163–164
MySpace, 107–108, 241, 243

National Sales Meeting, 233
National Speakers Association, 184
Native Americans, 131
NBC, 35

Negotiation
building alliances and, 101–103
protecting your value in, 158
question posing and, 138
Nervousness, presentations and, 180–182
Networking resources, 240–242
Networking sites, 107–108

Omni Hotel, 233
Operating Costs, positioning and reduced, 71
Opportunity
persuasive communication and assessing, 186–188, 191–194
zone of, 130
Optimism, 19–21
Options, presenting the, 200–202
Orientation. *See* Purpose orientation; Task orientation
Original equipment manufacturer (OEM), 228
Outcomes
aligning personal with customer, 11
identifying desired, 10–11
leading with, 7–8
outcome orientation (*see* Purpose orientation)
selling, 6–7

Pain, personal growth and, 20
Parinello, Al, 49–50
Paul, Glen, 228–229
Perceived Value (PV), 36–37, 153–154
Perseverance, 19–20
Personal growth, 18–20
Philosophy, sales, 124
Photographs, persuasive communication and, 203
Pictures, persuasive communication and, 203
Plaxo, 107–108, 241
Positioning
Commitment Sheet, 87, 88
overview, 32–33, 59–60, 87
strategic, 60–64
looking phase, 66–67
"no need" response, 64–66
tactical, 67–68
product or service, 69–70
resource, 70–72
title, 68–69
visualization and improving, 53
See also Global Resource Proclamation; Resource Proclamation; Situational Resource Proclamation